Table of Contents

Introduction 1

    Getting Started with Visual Studio 1

    Hello World – The Red Green Application 1

Doing the Math 7

    Variables and Operators 7

        Mathematical Operators 7

    Variables 7

        Naming Rules 8

        Basic Data Types 8

        Declaring Variables 11

        Assignment Statements 11

        Equations 11

        Temperature Conversion 12

Strings 14

    Length 15

    SubString 15

    ToUpper and ToLower 16

    IndexOf 16

    Concatenation operator 17

    Split 17

    ToString 18

    Converting Strings to Numbers 19

        Parse 20

        TryParse 20

Decisions 20

    Boolean Expressions 20

    If Statements 22

        One Line 22

        If/Else 22

        Complex and Nested If Statements 23

    Range Checking 23

Comparing Strings 24

Grade Reporting Project 24

Loops 26

    The basics 26

    Do/While 27

    For/Next.. 28

    Stopping the Infinite Loop 29

Fibonacci Sequence Project 30

Files... 31

File Dialog Boxes 32

StreamReader 33

    Read and ReadLine 33

    Peek 34

    Close 34

StreamWriter 34

    Write and WriteLine 35

    Flush 35

    Close 35

Files Review 36

Arrays.. 37

Array Properties and Methods 38

Multiple Dimension Arrays 38

Array Summary 40

Methods 41

Subroutines and Functions 41

    Functions 41

    Subroutine 42

    Method Parameters 43

    Scope of Variables 43

Arrays of Objects 46

Using arrays of objects 46

    Creating and Adding Event Handlers 47

Creating Arrays of objects dynamically 47

Objects and Classes 49

    Class Data 49

    Constructors 49

    Class Methods 50

    Class Properties 51

    Overriding Methods 51

    Declaring Objects 52

    Using Class Methods and Properties 52

    Objects and Classes Review 52

Fun Stuff 53

    Timers 53

        Useful Timer Suggestions 53

        Timing Window Problems 54

    Cursor Keys 54

    Moving Objects 55

    Collisions 56

    Images 57

        Open From a File Name 57

        Including Resource Images 58

    Menus 59

    Using Multiple Forms 61

        Sharing Data Across Forms 62

    Visual Studio Hints and Tricks 63

        Missing Windows 63

        Creating Event Handlers 64

        Advanced Editing 65

    Debugging 67

        Syntax Errors 67

        Logic Errors 68

        A final word on Debugging 69

Visual Basic Data Types 70

Installing Visual Studio at home 73

Index 74

Introduction

Getting Started with Visual Studio

Visual Studio is what is called an Interactive Development Environment or IDE. Visual Studio is a tool that helps a programmer develop computer programs in several different programming languages and for many different types of applications. This document specifically deals with classical Windows programs using the Visual Basic programming language.

Visual Studio is a serious professional development tool but still quite usable by beginners. In this chapter we will step though creating a simple project to work our way through using Visual Studio.

Hello World – The Red Green Application

Let's try things out to make sure everything works. First, we will create a new project. From the File menu select New Project

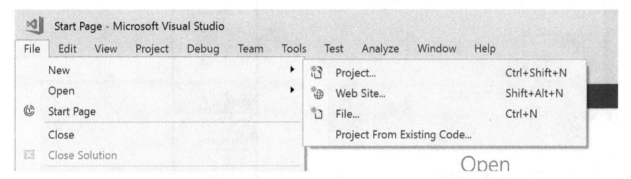

Make sure that the language selected is Visual Basic and that you have highlighted Windows Classic Desktop under the project type. Also highlight Windows Forms App (.NET Framework), and that your project is being saved in a known location. By default projects are stored in C:\Users\your user name\Documents\Visual Studio 2017\Projects) Also give your project a name – in this case RedGreen.

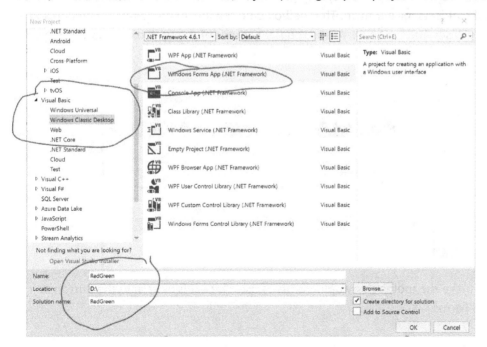

The name and location are critically important. Always make sure that you have created the right kind of project in the right location with the assigned name. Changing any of these things later is very difficult and sometimes impossible. You don't want to have to start over so pay attention.

Your project will open to something like the image below. The design window is where you will create the form for your project. Two important windows are on the right-hand side of the screen – the Solution Explorer keeps track of the files that make up your project and the properties window allows us to change how objects on the form look. We will spend a lot of time on properties.

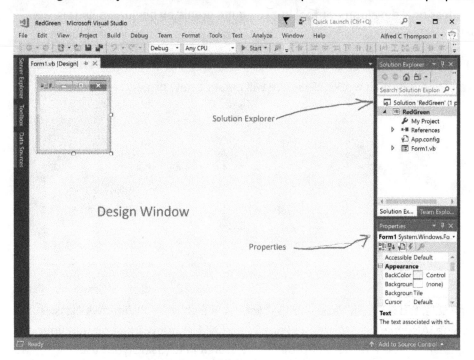

There is one more window we want to open before we go any further. This window is called the toolbox and it is where we find the objects for our form. The toolbox is on the left-hand side of the screen and when you click on it you will see your options. At the top right corner of the toolbox window is a tiny push pin icon.

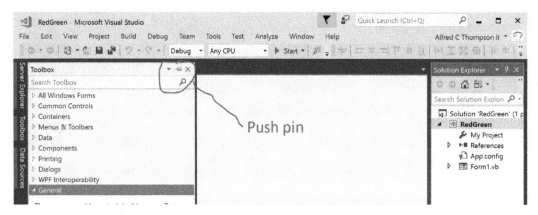

Click on that push pin to make the toolbox stay open for us to use. Once it is open find the Button object listed under All Windows Forms.

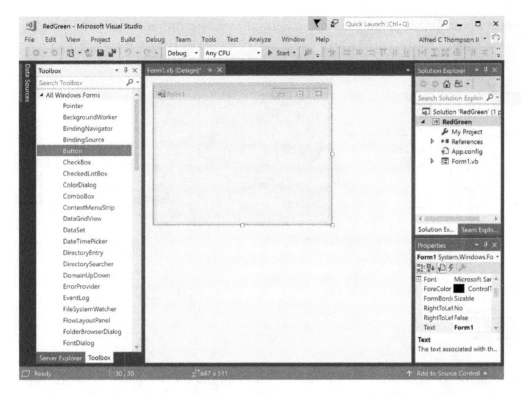

Drag the button from the tool box to the form twice. Or just double click the word button and a button will appear on the form. Once a button is on the form it may be dragged where ever you want it. We want two buttons for now.

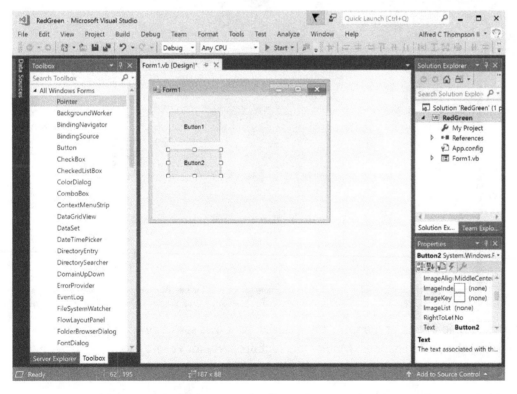

You can place the buttons anywhere on the form. You can also change their size by dragging the editing boxes at the corners and middle of the sides. Experiment a little until the form looks nice to you.

Names are important in a program. By default, these two buttons as named Button1 and Button2. These are not very informative names. The text displayed in them is not very useful either. These are both properties we can and should change.

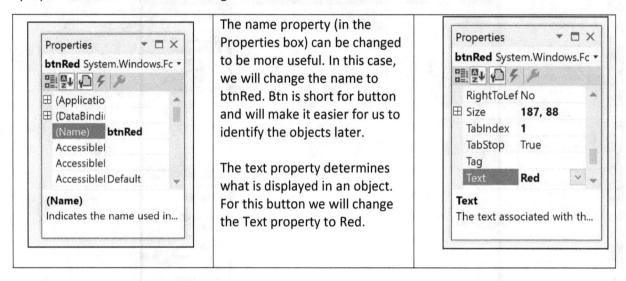

The name property (in the Properties box) can be changed to be more useful. In this case, we will change the name to btnRed. Btn is short for button and will make it easier for us to identify the objects later.

The text property determines what is displayed in an object. For this button we will change the Text property to Red.

After you do that, change the name of the second button to btnGreen and the text property to Green.

You can also change the Font property to make the words larger or to use a different font. Your project may look something like the image below but don't worry if it looks different.

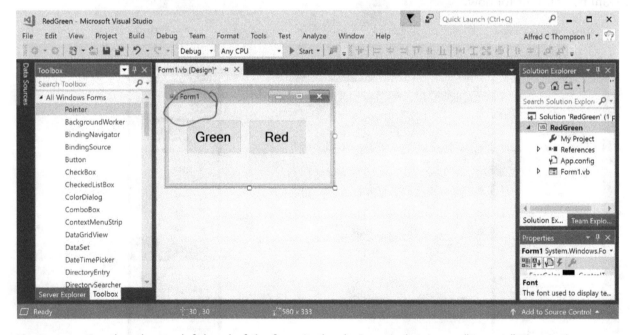

You may notice that the top left hand of the form in the design windows says "Form1." That is the default value and it really should be changed. Modify the Text property for Form1 to say "Red Green." **Do not change the name property!** Changing the name property can be tricky and is best avoided for now.

Now we are ready to write some code. Double click on the Green button and a code window will open. It should look like this.

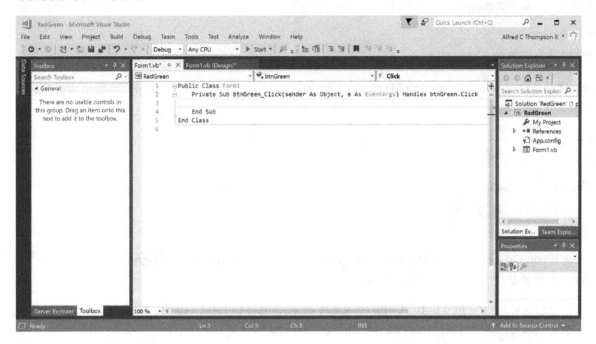

The development environment creates some code for us automatically. The code we have here is called an Event handler. As the name suggests this is where we write code that will respond to a specific event. In this case the code will be executed when someone clicks on btnGreen.

The form has a nickname called Me and a property called BackColor. We can change that property value by typing in the name (Me.BackColor) and assigning a new Color value to it. For example, Me.BackColor = Color.Green will change the color of the form to Green. You may notice that after you type Color. A list of possible colors appears. This feature is called IntelliSense and it very helpful for discovering new features and language functions.

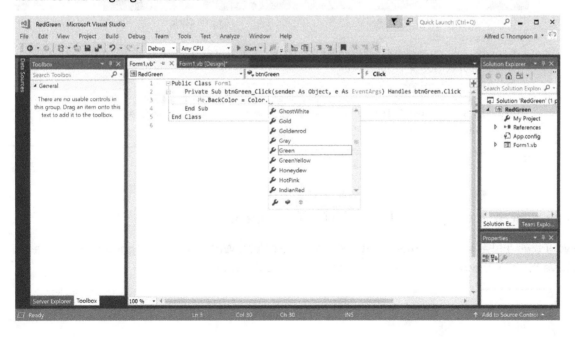

Time to test our program. At the top of the development environment is a little Start button.

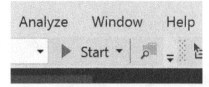

Push it and in a minute or so you should see your program running. Click on the Green button and see if the form changes color.

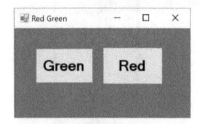

Hopefully, if you did everything right it worked. Now, shut down the redgreen program by clicking on the little X icon in the top right of the program.

Now let's add code for the Red button. The easy way to do this is to return to the design window (click on the design tab to do this) and then double click on the red button.

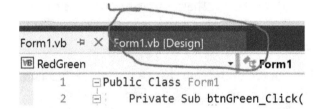

Here we will enter code to change the form to Red. You should have code that looks like this.

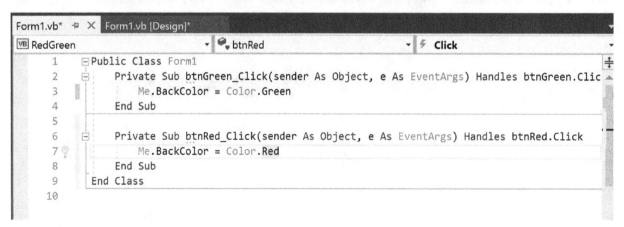

Test your program again. Can you switch back and forth from green to red?

Now on your own add at least two more buttons and more colors. What colors look good to you? The buttons have BackColor properties, does that suggest any modifications to you?

Doing the Math

Computers have been created to do mathematics from the beginning. The ENIAC was developed during the last days of World War II to do complex calculations. Mathematical calculations continue to be an essential part of computing.

Variables and Operators

While we can write computer programs with specific numbers in them, programs become a lot more valuable and flexible if we can have operations performed using different values. For this reason we use variables, named locations in memory, to make our programs better.

Mathematical Operators

Computer keyboards don't often have the same symbols we are used to using for all mathematical operators. The plus and minus are the same but we use the asterisk (*) is used for multiplication and the slash (/) is used for division. The caret (^) is used for exponentiation or raising a number to a power. Parentheses are used to insure a specific order of operations in an equation.

Symbol	Operation
+	addition
-	subtraction
*	multiplication
/	division
^	exponentiation
()	parentheses

Parentheses are particularly important to ensure that mathematical formulas are clear and understandable to both the computer and to people reading them in the code.

Variables

Variables represent locations in memory that store information. Each variable has a name that serves as the address for the location. Variable names should communicate information about the purpose and nature of the value stored in the location. The name of a variable is the first thing that is specified when a variable is declared.

Locations in memory are of different sizes depending on what information is stored there. This size is dependent on the type of the data. The computer will allocate the size of the location depending on the days the programmer specifies as part of the variable declaration.

The third critical piece of a variable is the actual information that is to be stored in the named location. This information can be specified either at the time a variable is declared or later via an assignment statement.

Important Reminder

Every variable has a name, a type and a value.

- What is it called? Name

- What kind of information is it? Type

- What is the information it is storing? Value

All three must be defined by the programmer!

Naming Rules

Variable names are one form of identifier. We will use names or identifiers for many types of objects, methods, variables, and program elements in computer programming. All identifiers in Visual Basic have the same naming rules.

Names are made up of letters, numbers, and the underscore character. No other characters are permitted. Identifiers may not include spaces for example. The first character in an identifier must be either a letter or and underscore. Numbers may not be the first character in a name. Unlike some other programming languages, Visual Basic is not case sensitive. That means that an uppercase letter and a lower-case letter are the same letter when used in a name or identifier

There are certain keywords that are reserved to the programming language and may not be used as variable names. These words are highlighted in blue by the IDE.

It is a useful practice to give names to objects and variables that indicated their type and purpose. This is done in various ways and companies often have coding standards that specify how names are to be created. Naming objects, textboxes for example, with standard three letter abbreviations that indicate the type of object allows Intelligence to help you navigate through a list of objects easily. The following table lists some useful three letter abbreviations.

Object Type	Abbreviation
Button	btn
TextBox	txt
Label	lbl
ListBox	lst
CheckBox	chk
RadioButton	rdo
Integer	int
Double	dbl
String	str
Random	rnd
Boolean	bol

Basic Data Types

Computers use a wide variety of data types. Each type holds a different type of value depending on it size (the size of memory it uses) and how it is specified in software. The following table lists several common data types, their size in bits, and the range of values that that data type can hold.

Name	Bits	Range

Bit	1	0 or 1
Byte	8	-128 to 127
Unsigned Byte	8	0 to 255
Word	16	-32768 to 32767
Unsigned Word	16	0 to 65535
Long Word	32	-2,147,483,648 to 2,147,483,647
Single Precision Floating Point	32	-3.402823-E38 to 3.402823-E38
Double Precision Floating Point	64	-1.79769313486232-E308 and 1.79769313486232-E308

While the computer hardware, and the Visual Basic programming language, support many data types we will focus on a few of the more common data types for now. These types are called:

- Integer - Real numbers
- Double – Floating point numbers (numbers with a decimal point)
- Strings – groups of one or more characters
- Boolean – values that are either true or false
- Random – a special type that give us random values

Integers

There are several integer data types in Visual Basic. Int8 uses only 8 bits and can hold numbers between 127 and -128. Int16 uses 16 bits and can hold much larger real number values. The specific integer type we will use is called Integer and uses 32 bits and holds numbers into the billions.

Byte – Signed Integer

Sign	Data Value						
0	0	1	1	1	1	1	0

Bit 7   Bit 0

Word – Signed Integer

Sign	Data Value														
0	0	1	1	0	0	0	0	0	0	1	1	0	0	0	1

Bit 15   Bit 0

Doubles

For floating point numbers, numbers with a fractional part, we will use a type called simply Double. This is a double precision floating point number that uses 64 bits. One bit is a sign bit and the rest of the bits are split between the exponent and the fraction as shown in the figures below.

Single Precision Floating Point Numbers

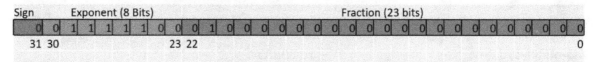

Double Precision Floating Point Numbers

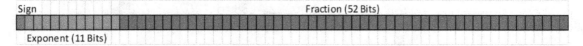

Strings

Strings are groups of characters. Each character, as are all values in the computer, is stored as a Binary value. When we declare to the program that a variable is a string it knows to treat that Binary value as a character according to a code value.

The figure below shows a selection of characters and their numeric value according to one coding standard – ASCII or the American Standard Code for Information Interchange.

Character	ASCII Value
A	65
a (Lower case)	97
(space)	32
5	53
@	64
Z	90
z (Lower Case)	122

Visual Basic also supports Unicode which is a much more extensive and powerful code that includes support for many more languages than just English.

Booleans

Boolean values are either true or false. Boolean variables are often used a flags or indicators.

Random

Randomness The quality or state of lacking a pattern or principle of organization; unpredictability.[1]

Random numbers generated by the computer are not completely random, but they are random enough for most purposes. We use them in games, in simulations, and any time we want to add some unpredictability to a program. The .NET Framework, supporting Visual Basic, provides a special class

---

[1] https://en.oxforddictionaries.com/definition/randomness

called **Random** that we can use. This object, when instantiated in a variable, provides us with random numbers of the type and range that we specify.

Declaring Variables

Declaring a Random Object

Objects of type Random are declared similarly to other objects by using the Dim statement with the inclusion of a New clause. For example:

```
Dim r As Random = New Random
```

Now that the object has been declared we can use it to get Random numbers.

Random .Next & .NextDouble

The Next method and the NextDouble method are used to return random numbers for use in a program. The default call (one with no parameters) returns a value between zero and the maximum integer value (0 to 2,147,483,647)

```
intCoin = r.Next()
```

A more common use of the Next method is to specify a maximum value for the random number. In that case, such as the example below, a number is returned that is between zero (may be zero) and one less than the maximum value specified by the parameter. The following example may return 0, 1, 2, 3, 4, or 5.

```
intCoin = r.Next(6)
```

The Next method with two parameters specifies the minimum value (1 in the example below) to return. The largest value will be one less than the value of the second parameter. This example may return any of 1, 2, 3, 4, 5, or 6.

```
intCoin = r.Next(1, 7)
```

The NextDouble method will return a floating-point value between 0.0 and 1.0.

```
dblCoin = r.NextDouble()
```

Generally, if a larger floating-point number is desired the value returned will be manipulated in some way depending on the number range desired.

Assignment Statements

One difference between equations in mathematics and computer programming is the purpose of the equal sign. In a computer program the equal sign is called the assignment operator. The assignment operator is a copy operator. In an assignment statement the value on the right side of the equal sign is copied into the location on the left side.

We saw this in the RedGreen program where the Color was copied into the property value for an object. These copy operations always copy from right to left.

Equations

Equations in programming are similar to those in math but just enough different to confuse things. Obviously, some mathematical symbols are the same as what you are used to. Addition is + and subtraction is -. The / is used for division but the * is used for multiplication. The multiplication symbol is not optional. You are probably used to writing something like 5(3 + 1) and seeing an assumed multiplication operator. The computer doesn't assume anything so that a programmer would have to write 5 * (3 + 1).

It is important to note that an equation in Visual Basic can only appear on the right hand side of an equal sign. That is because an equal sign in Visual Basic is an assignment or copy operation. In math an equal sign indicates that equations or values on either side have the same value.

The order of operations is also critically important in programming. The use of parentheses is important to indicate both to the computer and to people reading the code. Take a look at this equation:

$$4 + 4 * 4 - 4 / 4$$

What is the value? Because of the order of operations, the multiplication operation and the division operation are done before the addition or subtraction take place. The equation becomes:

$$4 + (4 * 4) - (4 / 4) \quad \text{or} \quad 4 + 16 - 1 \quad \text{or} \quad 19$$

Let's look at some more examples.

$$6 / 2 * (1 + 2)$$

$$6 / 2 * 1 + 2$$

$$6 / (2 * 1) + 2$$

How does the presence or absence of parentheses change the value of the equation? Does it always change the result? Remember that the computer processes operations of the same level or type from left to right.

Think carefully about how you express formulas taking into account the order of operations and use parentheses when necessary to make sure your intentions are clear.

Temperature Conversion

We are now going to create a simple program to convert temperatures from Fahrenheit to Celsius. You are probably familiar with the formulas.

$$C = 5 / 9 * (F - 32)$$
$$F = 9 / 5 * C + 32$$

We are going to create a program with two textboxes and two command buttons. We will change the name properties of the buttons and textboxes. We will also change the text properties of the command buttons and the form itself. **Do not change the Name property of the Form**.

Object	Property	Default Value	New Value
Textbox	Name	TextBox1	txtFahrenheit
Textbox	Name	TextBox2	txtCelsius
Button	Name	Button1	btnFtoC

Button	Text	Button1	F to C
Button	Name	Button2	btnCtoF
Button	Text	Button2	C to F
Form	Text	Form1	Temperature Conversion

Your completed form may look something like this:

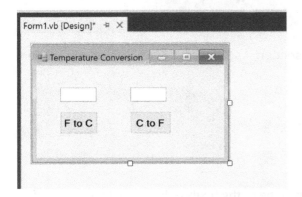

Now that our form is set up we can write some code to do our conversion. Double click on the button labeled F to C and the code window will be opened and look something like this:

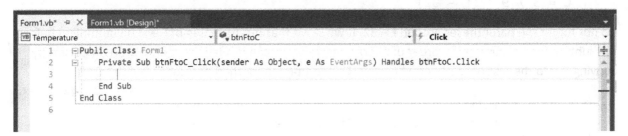

This code is the basics for what is called an event handler. This code will handle what happens when the button, btnFtoC is clicked. The first thing we want to do is to declare variables. For this project we will declare two double precision real number variables.

F to hold the temperature in Fahrenheit entered in txt Fahrenheit which will be stored in the Text property

C to hold the temperature in Celsius that we will calculate from the temperature in Fahrenheit. This value will be displayed using the Text property of the textbox called txt Celsius.

Our variable declarations will look something like this:

```
Temperature                                    Form1                         InitializeComponent
    1    Public Class Form1
    2        Private Sub btnFtoC_Click(sender As Object, e As EventArgs) Handles btnFtoC.Click
    3            Dim F As Double
    4            Dim C As Double
    5        End Sub
    6    End Class
    7
```

You will notice that there is a little green squiggly line under the F and the C. This is a warning that we have declared these variables but have not used them yet. Our next step then is to give these variables values.

The value for F will come from the textbox. The values in a Text property are strings not numbers even if we have typed only digits in them so we must convert the string to a number. Visual Basic has a function called Val that makes this easy for us.

```
VB Temperature                    ▾  btnFtoC                       ▾  ⨍ Click
    1      ⊟Public Class Form1
    2      ⊟    Private Sub btnFtoC_Click(sender As Object, e As EventArgs) Hand:
    3              Dim F As Double
    4              Dim C As Double
    5
    6              F = Val(txtFahrenheit.Text)
    7          End Sub
    8      End Class
```

Notice that we specify the Text property and not just the name of the textbox. We must be very specific like this for the computer. Now that we have a value for F we can calculate C.

```
C = 5 / 9 * (F - 32)
```

Do not forget the parentheses around F – 32. If we leave that out the value of F will be multiplied before the subtraction because of the order of operations. Now we can display the temperature in Celsius by copying it into the text property of txt Celsius. Our completed method now looks like this:

```
⊟Public Class Form1
⊟    Private Sub btnFtoC_Click(sender As Object, e As Ever
        Dim F As Double
        Dim C As Double

        F = Val(txtFahrenheit.Text)
        C = 5 / 9 * (F - 32)
        txtCelsius.Text = C
    End Sub
End Class
```

Now it is time to test our program. We should always test programs with questions we know the answers to in advance. For example, we know that 32 degrees is freezing in Fahrenheit while 0 degrees is freezing in Celsius. Similarly, 212 degrees is the boiling point of water and 100 degrees is the boiling point of water in Celsius. Just for fun, it turns out that -40 degrees is -40 degrees in both systems.

Try your program to see if it works. If it does not work, double check your equation.

Once your program works, on your own, write the code for converting degrees Celsius as entered in txtCelcius and displaying the converted to Fahrenheit in txtFahrenheit.

Strings

Strings deserve some special attention. Strings are a bit different from numeric variables. For one thing, they are variable in size. There are also some special methods and properties that make it easier for us to use strings in powerful ways. We also have a method, ToString, that all other objects and variables have that make it possible to get string information from them. In this chapter, we will learn about some of the more frequently used methods and properties that are supported by the String type.

The general format of methods is:

```
variableName.Method()
```

The general format of properties is:

```
variableName.Method
```

Note that methods have parentheses and may have parameters as well. Properties do not have parentheses or properties.

Length

The Length property returns the length of the string. This value can be saved as an integer value or used anywhere an integer value is appropriate.

For example:

```
Dim testString As String = "Garbage"
Dim count As Integer = testString.Length

For i As Integer = 0 To testString.Length
```

SubString

SubString is a method that extracts part of a string from a larger string. The result is a now string that is generally stored in a new string variable. There are two parameters used with the SubString method. The first parameter is required and indicates the index value of the string to start the substring. Remember that these indices start at zero so if you want the second character you would specify 1, 3 for the fourth character and so on. If there is no second parameter the substring that is created starts at the location indicated by the first parameter and continues to the end of the string.

For example, this code would create a new string that starts at index 4 and goes to the end of the original string.

```
Dim testString As String = "Garbage"
Dim myString As String = testString.Substring(4)
```

The value of myString after this code executes is "age" because we start at index 4 (the fifth letter) and get the rest of the string.

SubString – extracts a part of an existing string and copies it to a new string

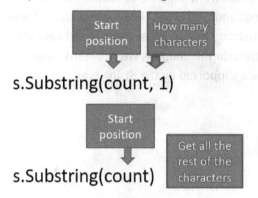

The second parameter (optional) specifies how many consecutive characters to extract from the string. Note that it does not specific the ending index. The ending index is calculated based on the length that the second parameter specifies. So for example, this code would return "bag."

```
Dim testString As String = "Garbage"
Dim myString As String = testString.Substring(3, 3)
```

If you specify a starting index that is a greater value than the length of the string you will get an error. Similarly, if you specify a length for the substring that would go beyond the length of the string you will also get an error.

ToUpper and ToLower

The **ToUpper** method makes all the letters in a string UPPER case letters. The **ToLower** method makes all the letters in a string lower case letters. For example:

```
Dim testString As String = "Garbage"
s1 = testString.ToUpper()    ' Becomes GARBAGE
s = testString.ToLower()     ' Becomes garbage
```

Notice that you must have a target string for the modified string but that target can also be the original variable. So testString = testString.ToLower() works just fine as the new lowercase string replaces the old string which many not have been all lower case letters.

IndexOf

There are times when you may need to search a string to find out if a specific character or group of characters is part of that string. The IndexOf method is used for this purpose. The IndexOf method has two parameters: The first parameter (required) indicates the string to look for in the string. The second parameter (optional) indicates what location in the string being searched to start the search just in case you do not want to start at the first character.

This code looks for the string "age" in the string textString.

```
Dim found As Integer = testString.IndexOf("age")
```

If the string is in testString, the value of found will be a number indicating the index of the start of the substring. In this case, that value will be 4. Remember that the index of the first character is zero! If the string we are looking for is not found than the value returned will be -1.

`IndexOf` and `SubString` are other used together. If you know where a string begins you can identify the characters before or after it for example.

Concatenation operator

The plus sign is also used as a concatenation operator. In other words, it is used to build larger strings from smaller strings.

```
Dim s As String
Dim x As String = "abc"
Dim y As String = "def"
s = x + y
```

```
s  ->  ""
x  ->  "abc"
y  ->  "def"
s  ->  "abcdef"
```

Integers and other non-string types must be converted to a string using the ToString method before being concatenated into a string! For example:

```
Dim output As String = "Demo number " + count.ToString()
```

There is more about ToString, including how to format information, below.

Split

The Split method splits a string into an array of strings. This is useful for parsing data that is read in as a group. We will see this again when we discuss Arrays and reading from files. The split method requires an array of string be declared to accept the results.

```
Dim s As String()
```

It also requires a string that includes a character that can be used to separate parts of the string. Common characters are spaces, commas, semi-colons, and slashes though any character is possible. The example string below uses spaces as separators.

```
Dim x As String = "a b c"
```

The format of the method is to assign the results of the split method to the array and passing a char parameter that is the separating character.

```
s = x.Split(" ")
```

Once the new string array is populated it can be used as any string array can be used. For example , the Length property will tell you how many elements are in the array.

ToString

Numbers are great for doing mathematics, but they are not the same as strings. For some operations, especially for displaying results, we want to convert numbers to strings. The ToString method converts a number to a string. Many things other than numbers support the ToString method but we'll leave that for later. The ToString method may be used without parameters in which case the system will display the number in the way it thinks is best.

For many numbers that default value works just fine. For very large numbers or very small numbers the computer may use scientific notation. That may or may not be what you want to display. For example, the following code converts from seconds to days and displays the result. One second is a very small part of a day.

```
Dim seconds As Double = 1
Dim Day As Double = seconds / 86400
lblOutput.Text = Day.ToString()
```

displays:

```
1.15740740740741E-05
```

We might want something different though. Perhaps something more like this:

```
0.00001157
```

Fortunately, the ToString method has a number of formatting options. We can build a string using a number of symbols to tell ToString how we actually want the number formatted.

Symbol	Meaning
0	Placeholder for a zero
#	Placeholder for a digit
.	Placeholder for a decimal point
,	Placeholder for a group separator
$	Or any other character – placed in that location

The second display above uses this formatting string as a parameter.

```
lblOutput.Text = Day.ToString("0.########")
```

This indicates that we always want a leading zero and that we want 8 digits to the right of the decimal point.

The hashmark (#) indicates the maximum number of digits to use when used on the right side of the decimal point. For example, this code

```
Dim pie As Double = 3.14159
lblOutput.Text = pie.ToString("##.###")
```

will display like this:

```
3.142
```

Notice that the right most digit is rounded up.

Larger numbers do not automatically include a comma or other separator. This code:

```
Dim bigNumber As Double = 1000345
lblOutput.Text = bigNumber.ToString()
```

Will display this:

```
1000345
```

Changing ToString as follows:

```
double bigNumber = 1000345
lblOutput.Text = bigNumber.ToString("#,###")
```

will give us this display:

```
1,000,345
```

For money, we might use a format like this one:

```
Dim pay As Double = 1234.56
lblOutput.Text = pay.ToString("$###,###.00")
```

```
$1,234.56
```

A little experimentation will help you determine what works for your specific application need.

Converting Strings to Numbers

String data and number data often look the same when displayed on the computer but are treated very differently internally to the computer. For example, the number 1 and the character 1 are stored as completely different values. The number one might be stored as 000 0001 but the character 1 will be stored as 0011 0001. Since these are clearly different values we must do some sort of conversion to use a string that looks like a number into an actual number. This operation is called parsing. Visual Basic has parse methods to convert from strings to specific numeric data types.

Parse

The Parse method converts a string to a number. This method is very simple to use. The format is

```
Variable = datatype.Parse(string)
```

The variable that the value will be assigned into must be the same data type as the datatype whose parse method we are using. The string parameter may be a variable, the text property of an object, or a literal string (characters inside quotation marks). For example, the code below declares an integer variable and uses the `Integer.Parse` method to convert the string value in a textbook text property into a usable number,

```
Dim n As Integer = Integer.Parse(TextBox1.Text)
```

Be aware that a program will give an error if the string does not hold a number. An empty string will be an error because an empty string is not a number. You need to be careful that only good data is passed into the method.

There is also a `Double.Parse` for converting strings to numbers with fractional parts.

TryParse

TryParse is similar in purpose to Parse in that it attempts to parse a string into a number. The big difference in result is that if it is unable to convert to a number because the data is bad a zero is returned in the variable. We also call this method differently.

For TryParse we do not use an assignment statement. We pass two parameters into the method. The first parameter is a string value while the second parameter is the name of a variable for the method to use to store the result of the parse operation.

```
Dim num As Integer
Integer.TryParse(TextBox1.Text, num)
```

Notice that the variable num must be declared before we use in the TryParse method.

There is also a `Double.TryParse` for converting strings to numbers with fractional parts.

Decisions

The most important difference between a computer and a calculator is that a computer can compare values and make decisions based on data or actions by users. In this section, we will look at how decisions are programmed in Visual Basic.

Boolean Expressions

Decisions of all types are made using something called Boolean Algebra. In this section we will be using Boolean expressions. These are something you do every day. For example, you answer true or false questions on a quiz.. You do more complicated Boolean Expressions as well. If someone calls all members of the girl's basketball team to report to the main lobby as student evaluates that as a Boolean expression. A boy would know they are not being called right away because they are not a girl. A girl would continue to evaluate and answer the question "Am I on the basketball team?" In all these cases we are looking for a true or false value to determine how to respond. More examples?

Is 18 greater than 19?

No, so that expression is false

Is 18 less than 19?

Yes, so that expression is true

We learned a bit about Boolean variables earlier in the book. Our code can check the value of a Boolean variable and take actions based on that. Our code can also create and evaluate an expression that includes variables and values to come to a Boolean result.

When creating these expressions, we use logical operators. Some of them you are probably familiar with though we express them slightly differently on the computer.

Symbol	Meaning
<	Less than
>	Greater than
<=	Less than or equals
>=	Greater than or equals
<>	Not equals
=	Equals
And	Both expressions must be true
Or	True if either expression is true
Not	Not tor or not false

Those symbols are used in a variety of ways and combinations. The result is always a true or false value.

Expression	Result
A > B	True if the value in A is greater than the value in B
A > B And B < C	True if the value in A is greater than the value in B AND the value in B is less than the value in C – both of the comparisons must be true for the whole expression to be true

A > B Or B < C	True if the value in A is greater than the value in B OR if the value in B is less than the value in C – only one of these two comparisons has to be true for the whole expression to me true
Not A	Assumes that A is a Boolean value if A = True then Not A = false. If A = false than Not A = true
A <= B	True if the value in A is the same or lower than the value in B

Those symbols are used in a variety of ways. The first things we will look at are called If statements.

If Statements

If statements are the basic form of decision structures for Visual Basic and many other programming languages. The basic format of an If statement includes a Boolean expression in between some keywords. If the expression evaluates to True a statement or group of statements is executed.

One Line

The most basic format of an If statement is:

If [Boolean expression] Then [statement]

With this single line `If` statement only one statement is executed if the Boolean expression is true. If the expression is false then the next line of code following the `If` statement is executed. It is not too often that we only want to have one statement executed for a true value. When we need several statements to execute we add the `End If` keywords to denote the end of a block of code to be executed and write our statement or statements between the `If` and the `End If`. For Example:

```
If e.KeyCode = Keys.Left Then
        Button1.Text = "Left" End If
Button1. End If
        Visible = True
    End If
```

The block of code between the `If`/`Then` line and the `End If` line can hold any number of statements. Even if only one statement is needed adding that statement between the `If`/`Then` line and the `End If` line can make explaining and enhancing code easier as a program develops.

If/Else

If we do nothing more, when the expression evaluates to false the next statement after the `End If` statement is executed. Sometimes though we want one thing to be done if the expression is true and something different if the expression evaluates to false. For this, we have the `Else` clause.

```
If Age >= 18 Then
    MessageBox.Show("You can vote!")
Else
    MessageBox.Show("You are too young to vote")
End If
```

One block of statements will be executed if the value of the variable Age is greater than or equal to 18. If the value of Age is less than 18 a different set of statements.

Complex and Nested If Statements

The real world is not always simply one thing or another though. For this we have the `ElseIf` statement.

```
If Age < 12 Then
    MessageBox.Show("Kids Price")
ElseIf Age > 65 Then
    MessageBox.Show("Senior Citizen Price")
Else
    MessageBox.Show("Regular Price")
End If
```

Besides using `ElseIf` statements, we have other options for more complex decision making. In the case of Visual Basic we have the ability of nesting if statements. That means that in one or more of the blocks of code a programming can include other If statements.

```
If  Age >= 12 And  Age < 65 Then
    MessageBox.Show("Regular Price")
    Else
      If Age < 12 Then
            MessageBox.Show("Kids price")
      Else
            MessageBox.Show("Senior citizen price")
      End If
End If
```

You will notice that there is indentation that the IDE adds automatically. This indentation helps the programmer visualize the nesting of statements.

Range Checking

Often you will want to determine if a number is without a specific range. For example, perhaps you want to determine is a person's age is in a youth group that is defined as ages 5 through 18. You know that this means that a value for age is greater than or equal to 5 AND that the value for age is less than or equal to 18. This would be expressed as (`age >= 5 And age <= 18`)

Avoid These Common Errors

In English, we might say something like "if age is greater than 12 and less than 65 …" and everyone would understand what we mean. The computer does not fill in the details the way people might. That means that an expression like "If Age >= 12 And < 65 Then" would not work. The compiler expects a value to be specified between the "And" and the less than sign.

A second way of doing range checking that looks logical to people but with means something completely different is the use of a dash. For example, "if age = 12 – 65" It is tempting to think that this means "if age is between 12 and 65 but the computer sees "if age equals 12 minus 65" which is something completely different.

Comparing Strings

Strings cannot be compared using the symbols that we use to compare numeric values. That is because strings are handled differently in some important ways that are mostly hidden from the casual programmer. Strings are compared using a CompareTo method. With the CompareTo method, we ask the system to look at two string values and tell us if they are the same or if one of them is greater (alphabetically) that the other. For example:

```
Dim myName As String = "Thompson"
Dim yourName As String = "Student"
Dim returnValue As Integer = myName.CompareTo(yourName)
```

The string myName is compared to the string value in yourName. The method returns a number value that indicates the relationship between the two strings.

Return Value	Description
0	strings are equal
-1	string parameter is greater in value than the calling string
1	string in parameter is lower in value than the calling string

In our example above, the value of returnValue would be 1 because "Thompson" is greater alphabetically than "Student."

Remember that this comparison is case sensitive. That means that uppercase and lowercase letters are not the same. This code below will not return a 0 because "Thompson" and "thompson" are not the same value.

```
Dim myName As String = "Thompson"
Dim yourName As String = "thompson"
Dim returnValue As Integer = myName.CompareTo(yourName)
```

The method can, as we did above, be stored in a variable. It can also be used by itself any place that a variable of type integer can be used. For example:

```
If (myName.CompareTo(yourName) = 0) Then
    lblOutput.Text = "We have the same name"
End If
```

Grade Reporting Project

In this project we will display letter grades based on the number grades that are entered by a user. We are going to create a program with two label boxes, a textbox and a command button. We will change the name properties of the button, label boxes and the textboxes. We will also change the text properties of the command button and the form itself. Do not change the Name property of the Form.

Object	Property	Default Value	New Value
Textbox	Name	TextBox1	txtInput
Label Box	Name	Label1	Label1
Label Box	Text	Label1	Enter a Grade:
Button	Text	Button1	Grade
Button	Name	Button2	btnGrade
Label Box	Name	Label2	LblAnswer
Label Box	Text	Label2	
Form	Text	Form1	Grades

Note that many people confuse the text and name properties because the system creates them with the same value by default. Changing the value of one of these properties does not change the value of the other.

Your form may look something like this:

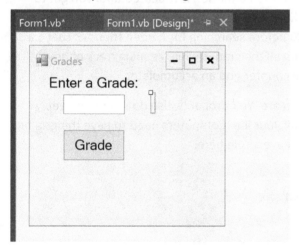

Double click on the Grade button and enter the following code in the event handler.

```
Dim intGrade As Integer = Val(txtInput.Text)

If intGrade >= 90 Then
    LblAnswer.Text = "A"
Else
    If intGrade >= 80 Then
        LblAnswer.Text = "B"
    Else
        If intGrade >= 70 Then
            LblAnswer.Text = "C"
        Else
            If intGrade >= 65 Then
                LblAnswer.Text = "D"
            Else
                LblAnswer.Text = "F"
            End If
        End If
```

```
            End If
      End If
```

Things to Notice:

- Lots of nested If statements – This is fine as long as there's an accompanying End If to close each If.
- There's no need to test "If intGrade < 65" for the grade of "F" - the Else clause of the previous If statement covers this.

Which is easier to understand? Which one is easier to modify and extend? It is always a good idea to think and several ways of writing a solution and keep in mind having to fix, modify, or extend later.

How might you do this differently? Try to add the "pluses and minuses." How much more code does that add?

Loops

You perform loops every day. Ever climb a set of stairs? The same motion is repeated until you get to the top. That's a loop. Ever count a handful of change? Keep counting until there are no more coins to count. Ever play a game where you counted to 10 or 100 before searching for hidden friends? That's a counting loop. Did you ever calculate your GPA? You total all the grades while keeping track of how many grades there are. You've performed a loop using a counter and an accumulator.

You probably do not think "hey, I'm doing a loop" but you are. You probably also do not think deeply about what is involved because you have been doing it all your life. Computers need to have things a bit more spelled out. And as we'll see, Boolean expressions have a role here.

The basics

At their heart, all loops have three essential components:

- Set up control conditions
- Check control conditions for completion
- Change control values

Just as we know where to start and know what will cause us to stop a looping operation in real life we have to make sure that the computer knows where to start and end.

In programming a loop, we have some variables or constants that we need to set before the loop starts. For a counting loop we will need a counting variable that will usually be set to zero. We need an ending value that will depend on the type of loop we are using.

Next, we need to use those variables and constants to determine if we are finished. For example, if I ask you to count some items you know to start at zero and add one for each item until there are no more items. If I ask you to hand me five objects you again know to start with zero objects and add objects until you get to five. We must specify this information a bit more deliberately to the computer than we do to people.

Lastly, something must change with our control conditions. In some cases, a counter variable must increase (or decrease). In some cases, we must have data that changes which we can check to see if it signals we are done.

26

Do/While

A Do/While loop is a loop that continues to execute while some condition is true. There is our Boolean expression again! A Do/While loop is set up something like this:

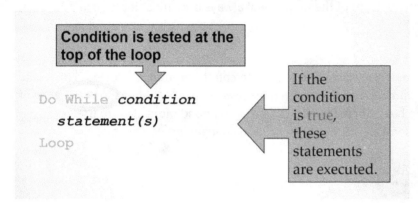

The key words Do While are followed by a condition – a Boolean expression – that evaluates to true or false. If the expression evaluates to true the statements between that line and the keyword Loop are executed. If the expression is false those statements are not executed. Because this expression is evaluated at the top of the loop it is possible that the loop's statements may not be executed at all. That is perfectly normal.

That condition is the check phase of the three essential elements of a loop. The next example, using actual code, shows all three essential parts.

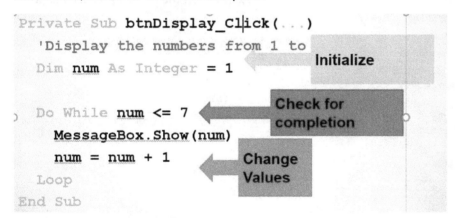

Our control value is called **num** and we are initializing it to 1. In our Do While statement we are checking to make sure the value of **num** is less than or equal to 7. Since we initialized **num** to be equal to 1 this condition is true and we execute the lines in the loop. One of the lines inside the loop adds 1 to the value of **num**. Without this statement the value would not change and the loop would never end. That would create what we call an infinite loop.

We can also check at the bottom of the loop. In this case the keyword Do is on a line by itself and the keyword While and it's Boolean expression are on the last line with the Loop keyword. For example:

```
Dim num As Integer = 1
Do
     num = num - 1
```

```
        MessageBox.Show(num)
    Loop While num > 4
```

Because we check our condition at the bottom of the loop, it will always execute at least once no matter what value we set **num** at initially.

For/Next

A counting loop is a loop that has a control variable that is used to count iterations of the loop. In Visual Basic these loops start with the keyword For and end with the keyword Next. A while loop can do all of the same things that a For/Next loop but a For/next loop can be simpler and more clear to use because all of the work of the three essential loop elements (set up, check, change) are done in one line.

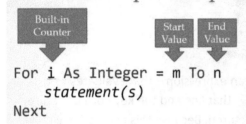

```
For i As Integer = m To n
    statement(s)
Next
```

In this example, we set the initial value (m) of our loop control variable (i) and specify that the loop will run until the value of i is equal to the value of n. Because we do not tell it otherwise, the value of i will be increased by 1 when the Next keyword like is reached.

Below we have two code examples that do the same thing. The example on the left uses a For/Next loop and the one on the right uses the Do/While loop.

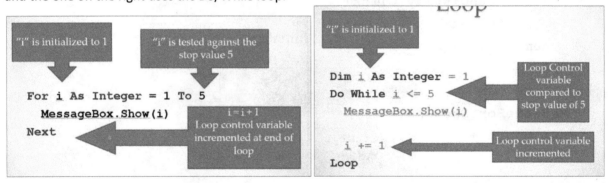

By default, after each pass through the loop the value of the counter variable increases by 1. There is an optional step clause that allows any number to be used as the increment. If the value of the increment is a negative number, the value of the counter variable will decrease after each pass.

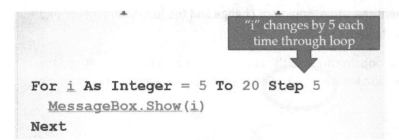

28

We can have a negative step value so that our loop can count down. For this loop to execute the statements inside of the loop the ending value must be lower than the starting value. You cannot count down to get to a larger number.

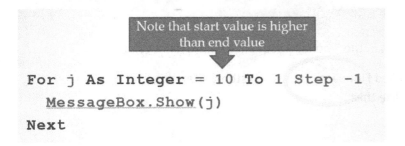

```
For j As Integer = 10 To 1 Step -1
   MessageBox.Show(j)
Next
```

Consider a loop beginning with

```
For i As Integer = m To n Step s
```

The loop will be executed exactly once if **m** equals **n** no matter what value **s** has.

The loop will not be executed at all if **m** is greater than **n** and **s** is positive, or if **m** is less than **n** and **s** is negative. If no Step value is given then the step used is 1 which is a positive value

One very important thing to remember is that For and Next statements must be paired.
If one is missing, the automatic syntax checker will complain with a wavy underline and a message such as
> *"A 'For' must be paired with a 'Next'."*

If you see this error message it means that you either have one more For statement than Next statements or more Next statements than For statements. This frequently happens when loops are nested – placed inside of each other.

The value of the counter variable should not be altered within the body of the loop. Doing so might cause the loop to repeat indefinitely or have an unpredictable number of repetitions.

So Don't do it!

Stopping the Infinite Loop

Creating an infinite loop is a very common error. While there are times when it is desirable those times are few and far between. When a program executes an infinite loop the computer appears to hang or stop working. We can usually stop a program in a loop though.

When an infinite loop is executing, the program can be terminated by clicking on the Stop Debugging button on the Toolbar (see the image on the right). You can also press the Shift and F5 keys at the same time or select the Stop Debugging option from the Debugging menu option.

Fibonacci Sequence Project

The Fibonacci sequence is a pattern of numbers where each number is the sum of the two preceding numbers, starting with 0 and 1:

0, 1, 1, 2, 3, 5, 8, 13 . . .

Write code to printout the first n numbers in the Fibonacci sequence where n is a value set by the user.

You will first need to create a project called Fibonacci and add a listbox, a textbox, and a command button. Your form will look something like this:

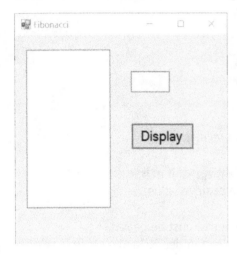

Change the names and text properties of some of these objects.
buttons and the form itself. Do not change the Name property of the Form.

Object	Property	Default Value	New Value
Textbox	Name	TextBox1	txtMax
List Box	Name	listBox1	lstAnswers
Button	Name	Button1	btnDisplay
Button	Text	Button1	Display
Form	Text	Form1	Fibonacci Sequence

Your form may look something like this:

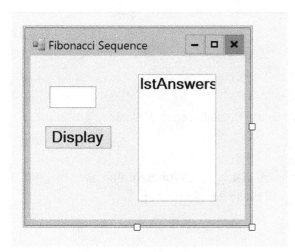

Double click on the command button and use the code below to get started.

```
' Declare some initial variables and their values
Dim one As Integer = 0
Dim two As Integer = 1
Dim t As Integer = 0

' Clear the display in the listbox
lstAnswers.Items.Clear()

' Get the number of numbers to display from the textBox
Dim n As Integer = Val(txtMax.Text)

' Display the first two numbers of the sequence
lstAnswers.Items.Add(one.ToString())
lstAnswers.Items.Add(two.ToString())
' write the loop statement here
' start of loop
    t = one + two
    one = two
    two = t
    lstAnswers.Items.Add(t.ToString())
' End of loop
```

What should the loop look like? Should it be a for loop or a while loop? Either will work here. The important thing is to correctly use the value stored in n as copied from the textbox. Before the loop we are already displaying the first two values. That is something to consider with our loop as well.

Files

Computer programs often become a lot more useful when they are used to process large amounts of data. Often this data is stored in files on hard drives. In this section, we will discuss how to read and write simple sequential files.

The .NET Framework has several very useful classes for reading and writing files. We want to add the System.IO library to the top of the program with the `Imports System.IO` directive to make these classes more easily accessible.

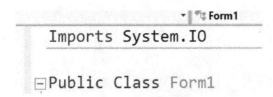

```
Imports System.IO

☐Public Class Form1
```

These "Imports" statements tell the system that we want to use these libraries of classes.

File Dialog Boxes

Two of the useful classes that are included in the IO library are dialog boxes for identifing files to opem for reading or writing. The Open File Dialog box is the first of these we will look at.

Our first step is to declare an object of type OpenFileDialog. As with any declaration we specify the type, a name and then create a new object using the new keyword.

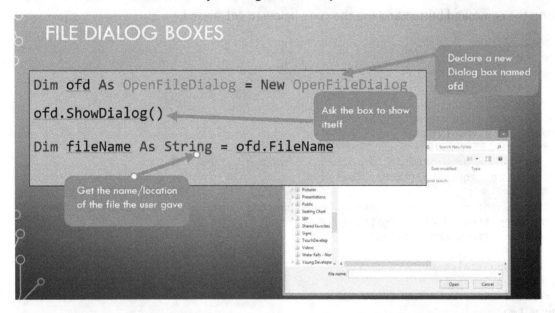

The ShowDialog command is used with the object we have declared to open the dialog with the user. The program will not continue until the dialog box is closed. When the Dialog box is closed and assuming that the user has selected a file the FileName parameter of our object will hold the full name and location of the file.

If we want to check to make sure that a file has been selected and that the user did not click on the Cancel button we will have the method return a value of DialogResult type.

```
Dim result As DialogResult = ofd.ShowDialog()
```

The return value can be checked in an if statement. Intellisence will show a list of options. Most often you will be looking to make sure that the user selected OK and not Cancel.

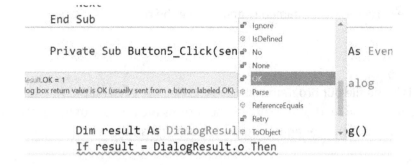

```
      End Sub

      Private Sub Button5_Click(sen    As Even

      Dim result As DialogResul    g()
      If result = DialogResult.o Then
```

The `SaveFileDialog` class is used in much the same way.

```
Dim sfd As SaveFileDialog = New SaveFileDialog

Dim result As DialogResult = sfd.ShowDialog()
If result = DialogResult.OK Then
    Dim fileName As String = sfd.FileName
End If
```

There are many options for these dialog boxes that we are not covering. You can learn more about them online:

SaveFileDialog Class

https://msdn.microsoft.com/en-us/library/system.windows.forms.savefiledialog(v=vs.110).aspx

OpenFileDialog Class

https://msdn.microsoft.com/en-us/library/system.windows.forms.openfiledialog(v=vs.110).aspx

StreamReader

`StreamReader` is the class we will be using to read sequential files. There are several important methods we will be using. The first thing we need to do is to open the file. That requires that we know the full name and address of the file. As we saw earlier we can use the open file dialog box to allow the user to specify the file. We can also have the name and location in a string variable or constant. Fully qualified file names include a device (disk drive usually), folders, and the file name and extension.

Files are opened for reading by declaring a new `StreamReader` object and specifying the file name in the parameter for the call to the `StreamReader` constructor.

```
Dim sr As StreamReader = New StreamReader(fileName)
```

Read and ReadLine

The `Read` and `ReadLine` methods are using to read the data in the file. The Read method reads the next unread character. The `ReadLine` method reads the whole next unread line in the file. The `Read` method returns an `int` value. The `ReadLine` method returns a string. For most beginner purposes `ReadLine` will be sufficient.

```
line = sr.ReadLine
```

In this example, we are reading from the `StreamReader` named sr and storing the result in the string variable `line`.

Peek

If we attempt to read more data than is in the file our program will give an error. The `Peek` method allows us to determine if there is more data to be read. The `Peek` method returns the number of bytes of data remaining to be read. If this value is greater than or equal to 0 we can safely read the file.

```
While sr.Peek >= 0
    line = sr.ReadLine
    ' process data here
End While
```

Close

When we are finished using a file we should always close it. By closing a file we allow other applications to have access to the file. It is locked against others while our application has it open.

```
sr.Close()
```

Putting everything together, we have code that looks something like this:

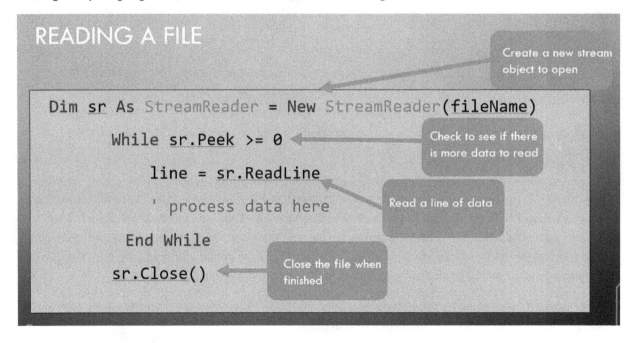

StreamWriter

The `StreamWriter` object is used to write sequential files. As with the `StreamWriter` object the program needs to specify the name and location of the file.

```
Dim result As DialogResult = sfd.ShowDialog()
If result = DialogResult.OK Then
    filename = sfd.FileName
```

```
        End If

        Dim outputFile As StreamWriter = New StreamWriter(fileName)
```

Note that if you try to save to a file that already exists you will get a warning before the file is opened and written into.

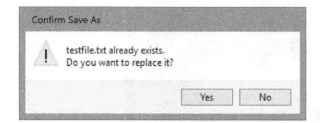

If the user clicks on the "Yes" button the file will be replaced, and old information will be lost. If the user clicks on the "No" button they will be returned to the save file dialog box for a new file selection.

Write and WriteLine

`Write` will output a single character or a string to a file. The location for the next item to be written will be on the same line as what is written with the `Write` method.

The `WriteLine` outputs data to the file and writes an end of line marker. The next `Write` or `WriteLine` will output to a new line in the file.

Flush

It is not efficient to write small amounts of data do an output device. Disk drives, for example, are most efficient when a whole block of data is written at a time. These blocks can be very large and contain several lines of data from our program. The input/output system buffers data or stores data in memory until a full block is ready. When the block is full then, and only then, is all the data physically written to the output device. The Flush command tells the system to write the buffer of information to the output device even if the buffer is not full.

This command is typically used when some time will take place before the next data is collected and ready to be written to the buffer. By flushing the data the program ensures that the data is on the output device and will not be lost if something bad happens to the computer or the application before the file is closed.

Close

When we are finished using a file we should always close it. By closing a file we allow other applications to have access to the file. It is locked against others while our application has it open. The Close method also makes sure that any data in the output buffer is written out to the output device or disk.

Put it all together and you have code like the example below which creates a 25,000 line file of "test data"

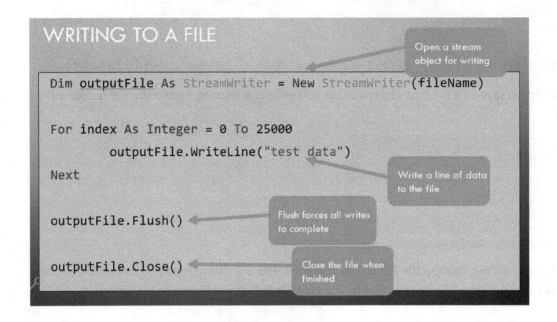

WRITING TO A FILE

Open a stream object for writing

```
Dim outputFile As StreamWriter = New StreamWriter(fileName)

For index As Integer = 0 To 25000
        outputFile.WriteLine("test data")
Next
```
Write a line of data to the file

```
outputFile.Flush()
```
Flush forces all writes to complete

```
outputFile.Close()
```
Close the file when finished

Files Review

- Include `Imports System.IO` to make sure IO class libraries are available
- Use the StreamWriter class to write sequential text files
- Use the StreamReader class to read sequential text files
- Specify file name and location of the file completely in the object declaration
- Use the .Write method to write data and leave a mark on the same line
- Use the .WriteLine method to write data and have next data on a new line
- Use the .ReadLine method to read a whole line of data
- Use the .Read method to read a single character as an integer at a time
- Use the .Peek method to see if more data remains to be read
- Use the .Close method to release the file when you are finished with it

Arrays

Imagine we want to analyze a set of quiz grades. We could have one variable for each quiz grade. They could be something like: Quiz1, Quiz2, Quiz3, and so on. This would work but processing could get complicated very quickly. How would you write an if statement to determine which quiz had the higher grade? How would you determine the average of the quizzes? Something like average = (Quiz1+Quiz2+Quiz3)/3.0 would work fine but suppose there were 10 quizzes? Or 100? Or a 1,000? The fun fades quickly. For this kind of situation, we have arrays.

An array has a name and a type like the variables we have been using already but it also holds multiple values. Each value is referenced by an index.

Array of Integer

Data values	45	23	17	87	2
Index values	0	1	2	3	4

The index values, which indicate a specific location in the array, are all integers – no half way into a location. The index value of the first element is 0. This means that a 5-element array starts with an index of 0 and ends with an index of 4. This may take some getting used to as we typically start counting at 1. If you remember that the highest index is one less than the number of elements you should be ok.

Arrays are declared similarly to other variables with some important differences. The usual naming rules apply and we still specify the type. We use parentheses between the type and the name to let the system know we are declaring an array. We must also declare how many elements are in the array. Visual Basic arrays start with an index value of 0. We specify the highest index value so a five-element array starts with an index of zero and ends with an index of 4.

```
Dim variable(highest index of array) as type
```

We must also initialize (set to a known value) all the elements in the array before we use them. We can declare and initialize values in one line or several depending on our needs. For example:

```
' Declares an array of integers without saying how many elements
Dim numbers() As Integer

Dim numbers(5) As Integer    ' Declares an array of six integers

' Declares an Integer array with 4 values - 3, 5, 6, And 2
Dim numbers = New Integer() {3, 5, 6, 2}
```

Here are some additional examples:

```
Dim numbers()              ' Declare numbers As an int array Of any size
Dim number(10) As Integer       ' number is an 11-element array
Dim i As Integer = number.Length
' Change the size of an existing array to 21 elements and retain the current values.
ReDim Preserve numbers(20)
' Redefine the size of an existing array and reset the values.
ReDim numbers(15)
```

```
Dim s(10) As String        ' 11 element String array
' Declare and initialize a five-element array
Dim numberz = New Integer(4) {1, 2, 3, 4, 5}

Dim names = New String(2) {"Matt", "Joanne", "Robert"}
Dim myNumbers = {1, 2, 3, 4, 5}     ' 5-element array With values
Dim myString = {"Tom", "Jane", "George"}     ' Declare and initialize a string array
```

Since we have integer index values we can easily use loops with our arrays. This makes it easy to initialize or analyze our values. For example, this loop sets all the elements in an array to zero.

```
Dim quizzes(9) As Integer
For index As Integer = 0 To 9
    quizzes(index) = 0
Next index
```

Using the loop control value as the index makes processing easy.

Array Properties and Methods

Arrays are objects which means they have methods and properties that handle common tasks for the programmer. Perhaps the most commonly used of these properties is the Length property. The Length returns the number of the elements in the array. Remember that this is a count of the elements and not the number of the highest index of the array. Using the Length property can help us to avoid off by one errors in loops. If we rewrite the loop from the last section to use the length property we can avoid many problems.

```
For index As Integer = 0 To quizzes.Length - 1
    quizzes(index) = 0
Next index
```

We use the length minus 1 because the highest index value is one less than the length because our first index value is zero.

The following table highlights several other useful methods for arrays.

Method	Description	Code Example
Average	Returns the average of values in a numeric array as a value of type double	`averageQuiz = quizzes.Average()`
Min	Returns the smallest value in a numeric array	`minQuiz = quizzes.Min()`
Max	Returns the largest value in a numeric array	`maxQuiz = quizzes.Max()`
Sort	Sorts an array by its values from lowest to highest	`Array.Sort(quizzes)`

Multiple Dimension Arrays

The arrays we have looked at so far are referred to as single dimension arrays. There is one index and we visualize these arrays as a straight line of values.

38

```
Dim PushMe(9) As Button
```

| 0 | 1 | 2 | 3 | 4 | 5 | 6 | 7 | 8 | 9 |

We can create arrays with multiple dimensions -two (or more) indexes. For a two dimensional array, think grids with x and y coordinates. We declare them with the size of the two dimensions.

```
Dim grid(7, 7) As Button
```

0,0	1,0	2,0	3,0	4,0	5,0	6,0
0,1	1,1	2,1	3,1	4,1	5,1	6,1
0,2	1,2	2,2	3,2	4,2	5,2	6,2
0,3	1,3	2,3	3,3	4,3	5,3	6,3
0,4	1,4	2,4	3,4	4,4	5,4	6,4
0,5	1,5	2,5	3,5	4,5	5,5	6,5
0,6	1,6	2,6	3,6	4,6	5,6	6,6

Three-dimensional arrays are declared with three index values.

```
Dim cube(3, 5, 5) As Integer
```

A three-dimension array might be visualized like this.

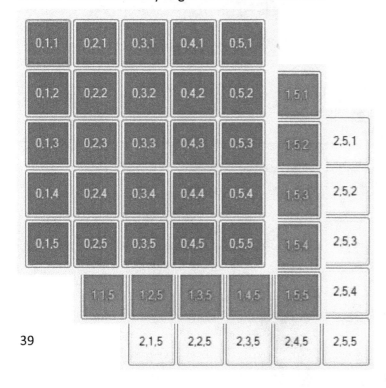

Working with multi dimension arrays is more complicated than a single dimension array but is generally worth the work when they are required. Remember that you must use all the dimensions when addressing an element in any array. For example, as in initializing the three-dimension array above.

```
For i As Integer = 0 To 2
    For j As Integer = 0 To 4
        For k As Integer = 0 To 4
            cube(i, j, k) = 0
        Next k
    Next J
Next i
```

Array Summary
- Arrays are a collection of values of the same type
- Elements in the array are accessed using an index
- Indices start counting at zero
- The largest index of an array is one less than the number of elements in the array
- Loops and arrays are natural allies
- Powerful properties and methods make many things easier

Methods

Subroutines and Functions

Methods, subroutines, and functions are all names for units of code that perform a specific set of instructions. Method is a more general term for these while subroutines and functions have slight but important differences in Visual Basic. The difference is broadly that functions return a value and subroutines perform their actions without returning a value. There are some syntactical differences as well.

Functions

Functions return values. The type of value to be returned is declared when the method is created. Methods may be private or public, a discussion we will get into more when we talk about classes but are most often declared as private. Just as variables have both a type and a name, functions must be named. Names follow the usual identifier rules (letters, numbers, underscores, no spaces) and should identify what the function does.

Functions may have parameters. Parameters specify the information that is passed into a function for it to use in its process. In the function definition, parameters are specified using their type and name. The values will be passed in when the function is called.

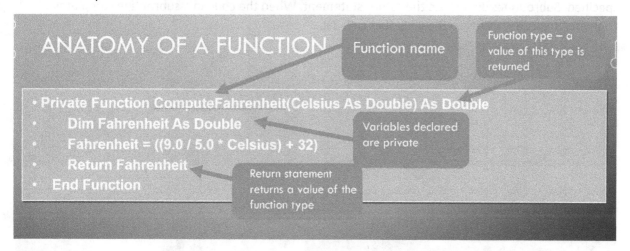

The function's return value is specified by a return statement. A function may have more than one return statement, but best practice is for there to be only one. Whether there are one or more return statements every code path through the function must reach a return statement.

Our example below shows a function of type string (which means a string value must be returned) and has a Boolean value as its parameter.

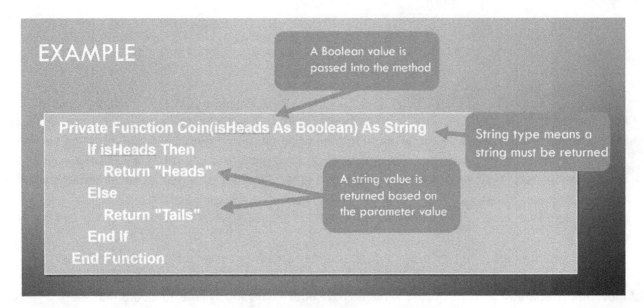

When the code in a function completes by executing a return statement, control of the code reverts to the code that called it and the return value is available for use at that location.

Subroutine

Subroutines do not return a value. Subroutines are declared using the Sub keyword and no type is specified. Subroutines do not use the return statement. When the code in a subroutine completes control of the code reverts to the code that called it.

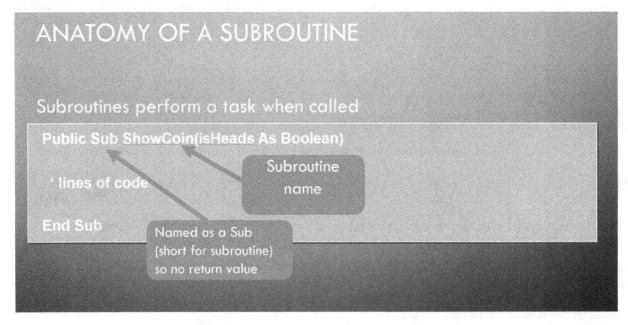

In this code sample, the void method or subroutine accepts no parameters but does some calculation and displays a message in a TextBox. You will notice that this subroutine calls the Coin function that we saw in the last section. The string value returned by the Coin function is displayed.

```
Public Sub ShowCoin()
    Dim toss As Boolean = True
    Dim r As Random = New Random()
    If (r.Next() Mod 2 = 0) Then
        toss = False
    End If
    TextBox1.Text = Coin(toss)
End Sub
```

Method Parameters

Programmers use parameters to pass information into methods – both functions and subroutines. Parameters are not required but most methods have them. Parameters make methods more flexible and powerful.

When a method is declared the type and name of each parameter is specified. The name of the parameter is used (and visible) only inside the method. The code that calls the method can and usually will use different variable names. What is important is that the same type of information is passed in the same order as in the declaration. If the method is expecting a string value followed by a Boolean value the calling code must pass a string and a Boolean in that order. The system will not rearrange things to fit.

Scope of Variables

The term scope in programming refers to where and for how long a variable is accessible. There are three basic areas of scope.

- Class-level Scope – exists throughout the class
- Method-level Scope – exists only in the module
- Block-level Scope – exists only within a block

Method-level Scope

When a variable is declared inside a method (subroutine or function) it can only be used inside that method. Space is allocated when the method starts and given back to the system when the method terminates. This means that values in that variable are not retained between runs of the method.

Class-level Variables

Class variables are created when the class is created. For example, a form is a class and when variables are declared in the class but outside of any of the methods in the class space is allocated and remains allocated until the form is terminated.

Variables that are declared at the class or form level are visible and usable by any methods in the class. If a method changes the value of a class level variable that change is visible everywhere in the class.

Addressing Class-Level Variables

Modules can declare variables with the same name as form level variables. This is not recommended for most cases as it adds to confusion. If a module declares a variable with the same name as a form level variable, the programmer should use the keyword "Me" to identify the use of a class level variable. For example, Me.Apple identifies the variable Apple declared at the class level to differentiate it from the variable apple declared inside the subroutine.

```
Dim Apple As Integer = 5

Private Sub Button2_Click(sender As Object, e As EventArgs) Handles Button2.Click
    Dim apple As Double = 3.14159

    Dim x As Double = apple * Me.Apple

End Sub
```

Block-Level Scope

Block level scope is limited to the code block in which a variable is declared. A code block starts and ends with matching key words. For example, If and End If, Do While and Loop, and For and Next.

In the following example, Apple is declared inside the If block which means that code after the End If cannot access it.

```
Private Sub Button1_Click(sender As Object, e As EventArgs)
    Dim foo As Integer = Integer.Parse(TextBox1.Text)
    If foo > 6 Then
        Dim Apple As Integer = 6
        Apple = Apple + foo
    End If

    Dim orange As Integer = Apple
End Sub
```

Another common use for block level variables is in for loops. When a loop control variable is declared in the for statement its scope is entirely inside the loop. After the loop terminates the variable is deallocated (the memory is returned for other use) and the variable cannot be referenced again.

```
For index As Integer = 0 To 10
```

```
    orange = orange + index
Next
```

Trying to use index after this loop terminates will cause an error because the variable's memory has been returned to the system.

Arrays of Objects

Imagine that you have a program with 81 buttons on the form. They are named something like Button1 though Button81. How to you address specific boxes? We have seen this sort of question before with variables. Wouldn't it be helpful to have an array of objects? Fortunately, we can do just that. For example, we could declare an array of 81 buttons

```
Dim demoButtons(81) As Button
```

Now what?

It turns out that we can add existing objects to an array of that type.

```
Dim demoButtons(81) As Button

demoButtons(0) = Button1
demoButtons(1) = Button2
demoButtons(2) = Button3
```

This is not the most efficient operation in the world but it is an easy start. Let us look at how we can use this array of objects.

Using arrays of objects

With an array of objects, we can easily set properties in a loop.

```
For index As Integer = 0 To demoButtons.Length - 1
    demoButtons(index).Text = index.ToString()
Next
```

We can also have a single event handler that responds to any of the buttons that are clicked. Remember that event handlers receive information in two data types: object and EventArgs. We can create this event handler as a new subroutine and declare appropriate parameter types for the event to be handled. For most events, we need an Object parameter and a parameter of type EventArgs.

Before we can access all the information that is specific to the type of object that fired the event we have to do some housekeeping. Specifically, we must copy the Object value into the correct data type.

```
Private Sub DemoClick(sender As Object, e As EventArgs)
    Dim b As Button = sender
    b.Text = "Clicked"
End Sub
```

Once we have cast sender (Dim b As Button = sender) into b we can access any property or method supported by Button objects. We can address any of the buttons in our array just as we address any similar object that is not in an array.

Creating and Adding Event Handlers

Event handlers are automatically created when we double click on objects on a form. Since we are adding these objects dynamically when the program is running our event handlers must be coded by hand. These event handlers are created as `private Sub` methods. The name, as always, should be descriptive of the method's function. There are two required parameters whose types are `object` and `EventArgs`. The names for those parameters can be whatever you want them to be but it is good practice to use the standard "sender" and "e".

```
Private Sub DemoClick(sender As Object, e As EventArgs)
    Dim b As Button = sender
    b.Text = "Clicked"
End Sub
```

Once the code for the event handler is written, we can associate the event handler with our dynamically created object. We must specify the type of event to be handled, that we are creating and associating an event handler, and name the method that will be handling the event.

```
AddHandler demoButtons(index).Click, AddressOf DemoClick
```

This statement should be included with the other statements that declare and define the object when it is first created.

Creating Arrays of objects dynamically

Creating objects, especially large numbers of objects, on a form and then adding them to an array manually can be time consuming, tedious and error prone. Fortunately, we can also add objects under program control.

The first step in this process is to declare the array of the appropriate type.

```
Dim demoButtons(81) As Button
```

It is important to understand that this declaration does not create any objects. What it does is create a reference or rather a group of references to objects yet to be created. The individual objects must be created and have some of their properties defined before they can be used. In the sample code below, a loop is used to create and position objects on the form.

```
Dim demoButton(10) As Button

For index As Integer = 0 To demoButton.Length - 1
    demoButton(index) = New Button
    demoButton(index).Top = 200
    demoButton(index).Left = 20 + (myWidth * index)
    demoButton(index).Width = myWidth
    demoButton(index).Height = myHeight
    Me.Controls.Add(demoButton(index))
Next
```

The location (top and left properties) are declared first. This is an important step to prevent the objects from being placed at the same default location (one on top of each other). The height and width of each object is also declared in this loop. These values are based on previously declared variables to enable adjustments to be made more easily in the future.

The last statement in the loop (`Me.Controls.Add(demoButton(index))`) is critically important. This step finally tells the system that the object is part of the form and must be displayed.

Objects and Classes

We have been creating objects on forms and using data types that have methods and properties throughout this book. These objects are built from what are called classes. Classes are abstract definitions of what an object can do and values it can hold. These classes are a mix of code and data, much of which is hidden from us. Classes are general descriptions and objects are specific examples of a class. An object is defined as an instance of a class. The act of creating an object based on a class definition is called instantiation.

We do not really need to know how the code behind an object does what it does. We just need to know what it does and what information it needs. This is referred to as data hiding. The data in the class and some of the methods that act on it are hidden and protected.

Class Data

Classes and the objects that are created, or instantiated, use data. This data should not be directly accessible from other code. As a rule, Class data is private to protect it from unsafe manipulation. The data is modified only by methods within the class that are designed to handle it safely. These methods may be either public (usable by other code) or private (for use only inside the class).

```
Public Class Die
    Private _Face As Integer
    Private _Sides As Integer
```

In the code above, we see that the keyword `Private` is used to restrict access to our class data. We could declare it as public which would let it be accessed from code outside the class but that is poor practice and should be avoided. One coding standard, used here, is that private variable names start with underscore (_) to highlight that they are private. This is not required but sometimes it helps to avoid confusion.

Most of the private data is initialized when an object is instantiated from the class but sometimes default values are specified. Most values are declared in a constructor method.

Constructors

Constructors are methods in a class that set the initial state of an object. Before any variable in a class can be used it has to have values. Constructors are special methods that set these values and construct the object.

Constructors are always public though they may use some private methods. Constructors in Visual Basic are always given the name New.

```
Public Sub New()
    _Face = r.Next(6) + 1
    _Sides = 6
End Sub
```

```
Public Sub New(sides As Integer)
    _Face = r.Next(sides) + 1
    _Sides = sides
End Sub
```

We can, and often do, have multiple constructors. These constructors must all have different parameter lists. The parameter list is how the system identifies which constructor to use.

A constructor with no parameters is called a default constructor. While not required, it is often a good design to have a default constructor if objects are typically created a specific way. For example, the default constructor for a Die object might create a six-sided die with a random value between one and six.

Non-default constructors may create objects with a mix of default and specified values.

Class Methods

The data inside of an object is accessed using either a method like those we have used already or by a property. A property is a specific kind of method that either sets or returns a value. Data in a class should always be private and read or changed using code specific to the class. Methods may have parameter values to pass into the method.

Some data should not be allowed to be changed after the constructor creates an object. For example, the number of sides for a die should not be changed.

Methods in a class may be private for use within the class or public for communicating with code outside the class. Private methods like the one below are often called helper methods.

```
Private Sub ChangeValue()
    _Face = r.Next(_Sides) + 1
End Sub
```

Helper methods are often called by public methods. If the case of a Die class, there may be several places where a new value is set for the die. Having a helper method to make these changes insures that all methods change the value in the exact same way.

```
Public Function Roll() As Integer
    ChangeValue()
    Return _Face
End Function
```

Public methods are used to communicate with the program that uses objects of the class. They may or may not return values and they may or may not have parameters.

Class Properties

Properties are used to get or to set the value of data in the class. The Length property for string types is an example you have seen before. Properties can be read only – just have a get function, write only – just have a set function, or allow a value to be both read and write. Write only properties are very rare and seldom make sense.

The Set part of the property method must include a parameter that is the same type as the property. The value that is passed into the property is validated. In this case the value is checked to make sure that it is greater than 0 and that it is less than or equal to the number of sides as stored in the variable _sides.

```
Public Property Value As Integer
    Get
        Return _Face
    End Get
    Set(value As Integer)
        If (value > 0 And value <= _Sides) Then
            _Face = value
        End If
    End Set
End Property
```

A read only property would only have a get function and must be labeled as ReadOnly. It might look something like this:

```
Public ReadOnly Property FaceValue As Integer
    Get
        Return _Face
    End Get
End Property
```

The value returned in this case is that of the private value in the variable _value as indicated in the return statement.

Overriding Methods

All classes, including ones we write ourselves, are built on top of the base class called object. One thing this means is that they inherit certain methods from the base object. One of the methods our classes inherit is ToString. By default, the ToString method returns some information about the class itself. This is not always as useful as we would like. Fortunately, we can create our own ToString method. We declare this new version of ToString using the keyword Overrides. That tells the system that we have a new version that is to be used with our class.

```
Public Overrides Function ToString() As String
    Return _Face.ToString()
```

```
End Function
```

We can create several versions of `ToString` if we use different parameter lists for the definitions.

Declaring Objects

Programs must first declare a variable of the type of a class to use it. By declaring a variable, we are instantiating a new object. If no parameters are specified (see the first declaration in the image below) than the default constructor is used, and default values are set for all properties in the object. If parameters are specified, then the constructor whose parameter specification matches the data types being passed is used.

```
Dim dice As Die = New Die      ' Creates a 6 sided die (default)
Dim D12 As Die = New Die(12)   ' Creates a 12 sided die
```

Once the object has been instantiated the program can access the methods and properties of the object.

Just as you can have an array of built in data types and objects you have declare arrays of user created objects.

```
Dim dice(10) As Die ' An array of 11 dice
```

Using Class Methods and Properties

The methods that are defined in a class are called using the format: object dot method name. For example, a Die class may have a method called Roll that sets a new random value for the die.

```
D12.Roll()
```

The Roll method may also be of type `int` in which case it would return a value. It might return the new face value of the die after the roll.

```
Dim face as integer = Die6.Roll()
```

Properties do not require parentheses because they never have parameters. A property may be used to get a value from an object:

```
Dim x As Integer = D12.FaceValue
```

Or it may be used to set a value if the property has a set method associated with it.

```
myScore.Score = myScore.Score + 1
```

Notice that properties can be used the same ways as any "normal" variable can be used.

Objects and Classes Review
- An instance of a class is an object
- One or more constructors to set initial values
- Constructors are named New
- Access to data is limited and protected
- Classes can override the ToString method to create strings for the object

Fun Stuff

Timers

A timer is an object that allows the programmer to have code that executes whenever a specified time interval completes. The timer object is dragged onto a form but does not display on the form. Rather it appears at the bottom of the design window. See image below:

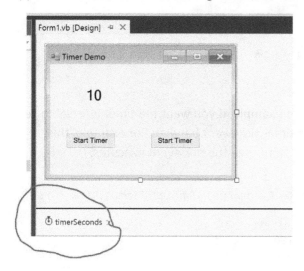

Several key parameters are important in using the timer object.

Enabled   True or False   Default is False

If the Enabled property is true than the timer is running and a timer tick event will happen each time the time interval is reached.

Interval   An integer value   Default is 100

The interval is the time in milliseconds (thousands of a second) A value of 100 is a tenth of a second.

Once the enabled property is set to true and tick event will occur every time the interval passes or until the timer enabled property is set to false.

Useful Timer Suggestions

Test your timer intervals. You may find that a tenth of a second (100 milliseconds) is a lot faster than you think or that 3 seconds (3000 milliseconds) is longer than you really want.

Think carefully about whether you want the timer enabled or not at the start of a program. A specific event (a menu or button selection perhaps) may be the way to go.

Setting the enabled property to the opposite of what it is can be useful for pausing or unpausing a game.

```
Timer2.Enabled = Not Timer2.Enabled
```

Having one timer with multiple counters running can be more efficient than having multiple timers. Multiple timers can cause timing problems as one timer may interrupt the code being executed by a different timer. This can be very difficult to debug.

Form level global variables (variables declared outside any of the methods) can be helpful. For example, if some events should happen every third time the timer tick event executes a global variable can be useful to keep track of these counts. For example:

```
Dim TimerTick As Integer = 0     ' Declare form level global variable

Private Sub Timer1_Tick(sender As Object, e As EventArgs) Handles Timer1.Tick
    TimerTick = TimerTick + 1
    If TimerTick = 3 Then
        ' do something specific for third tick
        TimerTick = 0    ' Set counter back to zero
    End If
End Sub
```

A timer can change its own interval or enabled status. For example, if you want the timer interval to get smaller over time you can decrease the value inside the timer tick event handler. For example, this sample speeds up the timer by a tenth of a second every third time the tick event executes.

```
Private Sub Timer1_Tick(sender As Object, e As EventArgs) Handles Timer1.Tick
    TimerTick = TimerTick + 1
    If TimerTick = 3 Then        ' Shorten timer interval by 1/10 th of a second
        Timer1.Interval = Timer1.Interval - 100
        TimerTick = 0    ' Set counter back to zero
    End If
End Sub
```

Timing Window Problems

Remember that even though the computer is very fast not everything happens instantaneously. If something in another part of the program takes longer than the timer interval it may be interrupted. While this is often desirable it is not always the case so be careful about long time running routines. It is especially important to make sure that the code inside the timer event handler is very fast so that it is not interrupted.

If the program or a method is going to turn the timer off, for example at the end of a game, it is a good idea to set the timer enabled property to false before any other end of program processing. If not you may see unexpected and undesirable interruptions in that processing.

Cursor Keys

Many applications respond to the pressing of various keys. The Arrow keys are especially popular for use in video games. A program can respond to KeyDown events on the form to enable this sort of activity. First, create an event handler for the form like this:

```
Private Sub PickBox(sender As Object, e As KeyEventArgs) Handles MyBase.KeyDown
End Sub
```

The new event handler must be connected to the program's form. See Creating Event Handlers for instructions on how to add a programmed event handle to an object, in this case the Form.

The `KeyEventArgs` value stored in **e** holds information about the key down event including which key has been pressed. The Keys object lists the various keys that are possible and can be used in an `If` statement to determine what to do. For example:

```
If e.KeyCode = Keys.Left Then
    Button1.Text = "Left"
    Button1.Visible = True
End If
```

Note that if there are objects on the form that can handle KeyDown events, such as textboxes, buttons, and several others, the form's KeyDown event may not handle the arrow keys as you would like.

Letters may still work however if you attach the same event handler to all objects on the form that handle KeyDown events. The combination of AWSD often substitutes for left, up, down and right respectively. As with many things, experimentation will help you understand how using these keys in your program will work.

For best results, you will want to limit enabled objects on the form to those that do not respond to KeyDown events. Examples of objects to use are labels and picture boxes.

If you want to use buttons or similar objects on your form and find that they "catch" the KeyDown events you can have them be disabled when not needed. For example, you may have a start button to start a game timer. Once the timer is enabled you should set the enabled property of the button to false. This will remove it from the form (really make it invisible) and allow KeyDown events to be handled by your movement code. You can set the enabled property back to true if you want the users to have access to it later.

Moving Objects

Objects can be moved by changing their Top and Left property values. One way to do this is in a timer event. The code below moves each of the two picture boxes over to the right by 15 pixels (the value set in the MoveMe variable) each time the timer fires.

```
Dim MoveMe As Integer = 15

Private Sub timer1_Tick(sender As Object, e As EventArgs) Handles timer1.Tick
    pictureBox1.Left = pictureBox1.Left + MoveMe
    pictureBox2.Left = pictureBox2.Left + MoveMe
End Sub
```

Increasing the value of the Top parameter would move the object down the form. To move the object right the value of the Left property would be decreased. Likewise, to move the object up the form the value of the Top property would be decreased.

By setting the top and left values, an object can be placed in any specific spot on the form.

One issue with moving objects is determining what happens when the object reaches the end of the form at the top, bottom, or one of the sides. Fortunately, these situations are easily detected. For example, the width of the form is easily determined as a property of the form. If a variable is used for the number of pixels to move (highly recommended) than checking to see if the object has moved too far right (its left value is greater than the width of the form) or too far to the left (the object's left value is less than zero) the number of spaces to move can be reversed.

```
Dim MoveMe As Integer = 15

Private Sub timer1_Tick(sender As Object, e As EventArgs) Handles timer1.Tick
    pictureBox1.Left = pictureBox1.Left + MoveMe
    If pictureBox1.Left > Me.Width Or pictureBox1.Left <= 0 Then
        MoveMe = MoveMe * -1
    End If
```

Just as the Left value can be checked against the width of the form, the Top value can be checked against the Height of the form.

If you want an object to move both up and down and left and right is can be useful to define a variable for each moving Top and moving Left.

```
Dim moveTop As Integer = 15
Dim moveLeft As Integer = 25
```

The two values do not have to be the same in will often be different. Now if you add code to move the objects and to change directions when the objects "hit a wall" you can have objects that "bounce."

```
PictureBox4.Top = PictureBox4.Top + moveTop
PictureBox4.Left = PictureBox4.Left + moveLeft
If PictureBox4.Left > Me.Width Or PictureBox4.Left < 0 Then
    moveLeft = moveLeft * -1
End If
If PictureBox4.Top > Me.Height Or PictureBox4.Top < 0 Then
    moveTop = moveTop * -1
End If
```

In this case, the object is likely to disappear briefly off to the left or down the bottom because we are checking the trailing edge not the leading edge. We may want to add the width or height of the object to fix this.

```
If PictureBox4.Left + PictureBox4.Width > Me.Width Or PictureBox4.Left < 0 Then
    moveLeft = moveLeft * -1
End If
If PictureBox4.Top + PictureBox4.Height > Me.Height Or PictureBox4.Top < 0 Then
    moveTop = moveTop * -1
End If
```

We can also determine if we are touching other objects on the form by comparing combinations of Top and Left but that can be complicated. In the next section, Collisions, we learn about a fairly simple way to detect when two objects come into contact or interact or collide.

Collisions

The .NET Framework has a special data type called Rectangle. A Rectangle object represents an area defined by its left and top location (or X and Y) and a height and width. Controls that appear on a form include a property called Bounds that is of type Rectangle. For our purposes, it is handy that the

`Rectangle` object has a method called `IntersectsWith` that we can use to ask the computer to determine if two rectangles overlap. All we need to do is use the results of a call to the Bounds properties of the two objects with the `IntersectsWith` method. The `IntersectsWith` method returns a Boolean value which we can use anywhere a Boolean expression is required – an `if` statement or a `while` loop for example.

In this example, we have two boxes – one of the left and one on the right of the form. As they move, we want to see if they collide.

```
if (pictureBox1.Bounds.IntersectsWith(pictureBox2.Bounds))
  ' Statements
End If
```

If the two rectangles overlap the method returns true and the statements inside the if statement are executed.

You can also define areas on a form as a rectangle. You may want to define a location on a form without having to create an object to sit there. You can use that Rectangle variable to move objects to the location or check that location to see if an object interests with it.

```
Dim myMarker As Rectangle = New Rectangle(myLeft, myTop, myWidth, myHeight)
```

Order is important here - X, Y, Width, Height – entering parameters in a different order will cause you problems and give you unexpected results.

Images

There are basically two ways to add images to an object in a Visual Basic program. One is to load a specific file using a fully specified filename. The other is to add an image to a project as a resource and use it from there.

The first way allows one to select an image at run-time by using an Open File Dialog box. Adding a specific filename to source code and using this method has some risk though as if a file moves or is renamed the program will generally fail to run. For images that will always be the same using a resource is more reliable.

Open From a File Name

The following code displays an Open File Dialog box and loads the image found into a picture box named picShow.

```
OpenFileDialog ofd = new OpenFileDialog()
ofd.ShowDialog()

picShow.Image = new Bitmap(ofd.FileName)
```

Including Resource Images

You can also create a resource file and load images into that file. Images in the resource file can be used in your program while it is executing.

First right click on the project name and select Add -> New Item

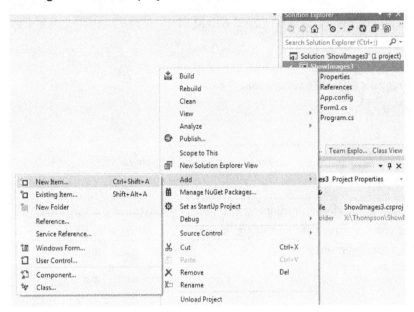

From the Add New Item dialog box find and select Resources File (you may have to scroll down a bit)

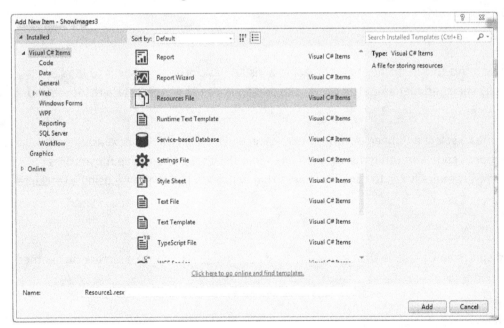

You can leave the default name (Resources1.resx) or change it. Be sure to leave the file extension as .resx however. From the Add Resources dialog select Add Existing File from the Add Resource tab.

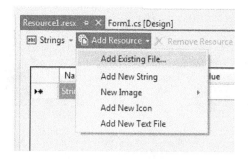

Browse to the image you want to include and click the Open button.

The image you want to use will appear in the resources box.

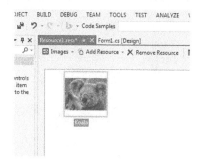

You can now load your image using a statement like this:

```
Me.BackgroundImage = Global.Arrows_VB.My.Resources.Resource1.Koala
```

In this case "ShowImages3" is the name of the project. Resource1 is the name of the resource file. Koala is the name of the image resource. Intellisence will help you with entering most of this after Global.

Note that you may want to modify the BackgroundImageLayout property. For example, the Stretch property will make the image fit into the available space on the object.

Menus

Most Windows program use menus for many setting and options. The .NET Framework that is supported by Visual Basic has a Menu object that may be added to your forms.

The first step is to drag the MenuStrip object to your form. Once the menu is on the form, you can type

 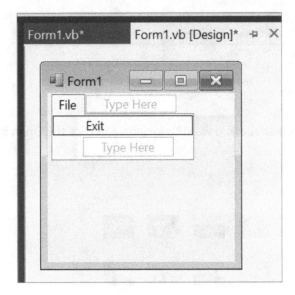

the descriptions of the various commands.

Double clicking on any of the menu items will open an event handler for that command. For example, an exit menu option might look something like this:

```
Private Sub ExitToolStripMenuItem_Click(sender As Object, e As EventArgs) Handles
                                        ExitToolStripMenuItem.Click
        Application.Exit()
End Sub
```

Using Multiple Forms

Go to the Project Menu and select Add Windows Form. Make sure that Windows Form is selected and give a meaningful name to your form.

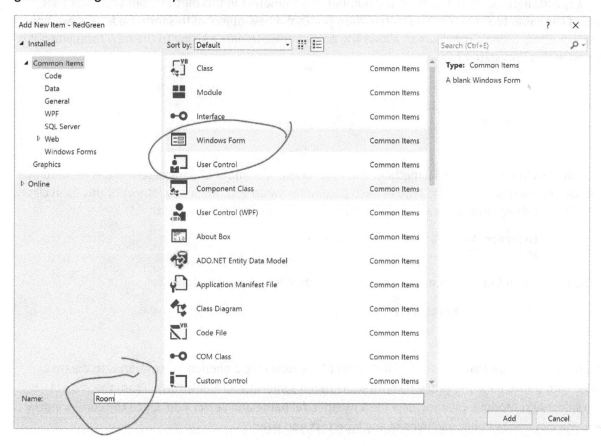

Inside your program, you can now declare a new object of the type form you have created.

```
Dim Entrance As Room = New Room
```

Declaring a form (called Entrance and of type Room in this example, does not display it. To do that you have to tell it to show itself. There are two ways to show a form – Show and ShowDialog. The Show method will display the form and move on to the next line of code.

```
Entrance.Show()
```

If you want the program to stop doing anything until the newly displayed form is closed use ShowDialog.

```
Entrance.ShowDialog()
```

If you want to have a new form open and make the form that loads it "go away" you can show the new form and hide the loading form.

```
                    Entrance.Show()
                    Me.Hide()
```

You can pass information to a new form by creating new constructors for the class. The method called `New` is a special method. You may have any number of parameters in this method, but you must pass values of the same type as each parameter when you Dim a new object of this form class. For example, this `New` method, called a constructor, allows the programmer to pass a string to the new form when it is declared with a Dim statement.

```
Public Class Room
    Public Sub New(Name As String)
        Me.Text = Name
    End Sub
End Class
```

The method called `New` is a special method. You may have any number of parameters in this method but you must pass values of the same type as each parameter when you Dim a new object of this form class. This will take a string parameter and use that to set the text property in the form:

```
Dim Entrance As Room = New Room("Demo")
Entrance.Show()
```

Use the Application.Exit comment to close the application when you are done.

```
        Application.Exit()
```

Sharing Data Across Forms

If you need data to be shared across all instances of the new forms opened one option is to create a module with public data. A module is created the much same way as a new form. From the Project Menu select Add Module. Give the new file a meaningful name and Select Add. Once the code window opens you can create Public variables of any type that you need.

```
1    Module GlobalVariables
2        Public gValue As String
3        Public gCount As Integer
4    End Module
5
```

Be sure that the variables are created using the `Public` key word. These variables can now be accessed (both read and modified) by any form in the project.

```
3
4            gValue = "Main Form"
5            gCount = 0
6
```

Any changes made to any of these variables will be visible in any form in the project and changes made in one form will persist as long as the project is running.

Visual Studio Hints and Tricks

Visual Studio can be complicated and confusing for beginners. In this section we will learn about several common issues for beginners and how to deal with them.

Missing Windows

The three most important windows that beginners delete are the Solution Explorer, which organizes the files in the project, the ToolBox, which holds the objects to be used on a form, and the Properties Window, which is used to set properties of objects on the form. Fortunately all of these windows can be recovered by using the correct option on the View menu as shown below.

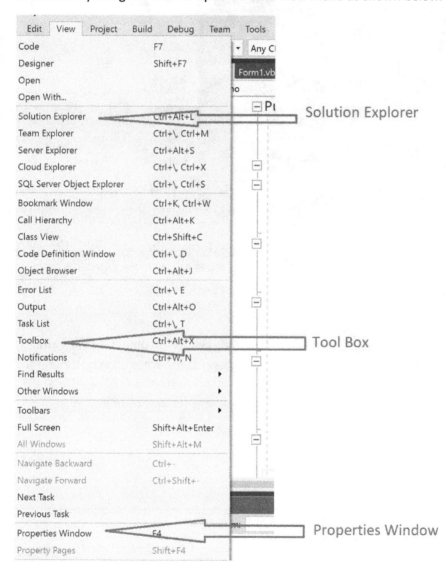

Sometimes you will open a project and the design window for the form is not displayed. This window can be called up by double clicking on the form in the Solution Explorer as in the image below.

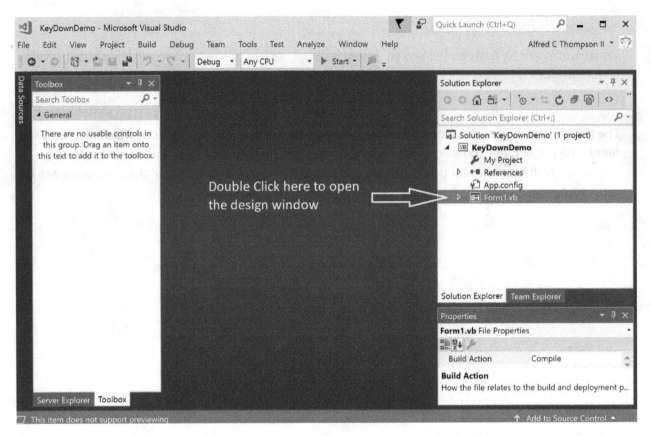

The code window can be opened by double clicking on any object on a form or the form itself. This will also create a new event handler which may not may not be wanted. If it is not wanted, you can simply delete it in Visual Basic projects.

Creating Event Handlers

While a programmer can easily create and event handler by double clicking on an object on the form. By default, this double click often creates an event handler for the click event. For other objects, these is a different default event handler created. Often you will want to create an even handler for a different event completely. A programmer may also want to discover the list of events that an object can respond to.

The lightning icon on the properties window will open a list of events for the currently selected object.

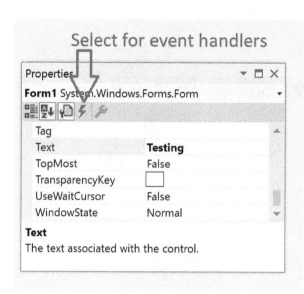

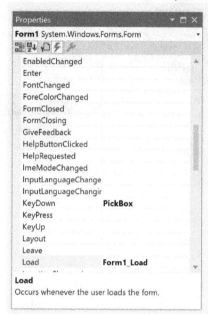

This list will show any event handlers that are already connected to the selected object. Selecting an event and clicking on the dropdown list icon will show you the event handlers that already exist, if any, that can respond to that event for that object.

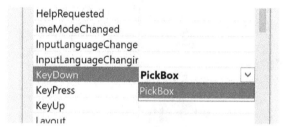

You can select one of those event handlers or type in the name of the event handler you want Visual Studio to create for that event. Double clicking on a listed event will create an event handler using the default naming conventions (usually object name, underscore, and the event name.)

Advanced Editing

The Edit menu has some very powerful options that can be very helpful for programmers. Under the Advanced option there are four that are of particular value to beginners. The first two are "Format Document" and "Format Selection." Normally, Visual Studio takes care of a lot of formatting. Line indentation is very helpful for understanding nesting and related logic issues. Sometimes the formatting is not done or becomes undone. The Format options tells Visual Studio to "clean up" the formatting.

This can make the code a lot easier to read. If there are syntax errors Visual Studio may not be able to format for you though so take care of those first.

Comment and uncomment selection tells Visual Studio to comment the section of code that you have selected. Using comments to temporarily remove statements from execution is a powerful debugging tool. Using Visual Studio to comment or uncomment a block of code is often faster and more reliable than doing so manually.

Debugging

Debugging is the process of finding and correcting problems or defects in a computer program. It can be a major problem for beginners. The two major categories of problems or bugs in programs are syntax errors and logic errors.

Syntax Errors

Syntax errors are errors that involve errors that are caught by the IDE before the program is executed. The IDE highlights these errors with a red squiggly line. The first step in correcting these errors is understanding what they are. Pointing at the red squiggly error with the cursor will cause a message to be displayed.

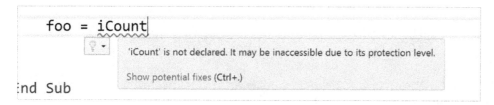

Clicking on "Show potential fixes" may provide additional information but is not always a sure fix. In the case of this example it is important to understand the scope of variables.

Warnings are indicated with a green squiggly line. Warnings may appear for simple things such as variables being declared but not used yet. Those will disappear when the variable is used.

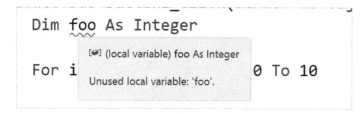

Other warnings may point out potential logical errors that will show up when the program is executed. Warnings, unlike errors, do not prevent the program from executing.

One of the most common warnings beginners see is from attempting to use a variable that has not had a value assigned. The warning message here is helpful.

```
For iCount = 0 To 10
    name = foo
Next
        [●] (local variable) foo As String

        Variable 'foo' is used before it has been assigned a value. A null reference exception could result at runtime.
```

t is often the case that one minor, or apparently minor, warning or error will create more errors further down in the program. One should not assume that the problem indicated is always with the line where it appears. If a problem is not obvious one should look at previous lines in the code.

Logic Errors

Logic errors are errors that do not keep the program from executing but cause it to give incorrect results. They could be as simple as an incorrect formula or a badly formed set of if statements. Simple to make does not always mean simple to find though.

Formulas should be looked at closely and worked through by hand to make sure they are accurate. This formula is missing some parentheses for example.

```
F = double.Parse(txtFahrenheit.Text);
C = 5.0 / 9.0 * F - 32;
txtCelsius.Text = C.ToString();
```

Formulas, like all processes, should be tested with known values with known results. For example:

Fahrenheit		Celsius
32	Freezing point of water	0
212	Boiling point of water	100
-40	Yes, they are the same	-40

Visual Studio has a debugging facility built into the system. Clicking on the gray bar to the left of a statement of code sets what is called a break point. (See figure below)

```
32
          Break point   for (int i = 0; i < number; i++)
34                       {
35                           output += "X";
36                           ListBox1.Items.Add(output);
37                       sw.WriteLine(output);
38
```

When the program is executed the debugger will stop execution when a break point is reached. The step into command (or F11 function key) will cause the program to execute one statement at a time.

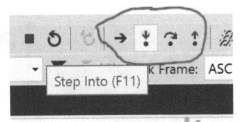

This will allow the programmer to verify the path the code is taking. This can be helpful to verify that loops are executed, if statements are evaluated as expected, or the code (such as an event handler) are reached as expected.

The debugger will also allow the programmer to check the values of variables as the program is executed.

Holding the cursor over variables will cause their present value to be displayed.

```
▶| output += "X";
    ListBox1.Items.Add(output);
```

These are only a few of the capabilities of the debugger and experimentation or exploration of the Visual Studio documentation is recommended.

A final word on Debugging

Do not hesitate to ask others for help. Be sure to explain the problem as well as what is supposed to be happening in the code. Take this advice from two of the most famous names in software.

> Another effective technique is to explain your code to someone else. This will often cause you to explain the bug to yourself. Sometimes it takes no more than a few sentences, followed by an embarrassed "Never mind, I see what's wrong. Sorry to bother you." This works remarkably well; you can even use non-programmers as listeners. One university computer center kept a teddy bear near the help desk. Students with mysterious bugs were required to explain them to the bear before they could speak to a human counselor. ~Brian Kernighan and Rob Pike, about debugging

Visual Basic Data Types

While this book focuses on several of the most commonly used data types there are many more supported by Visual Basic. The Table below from the official documentation (https://docs.microsoft.com/en-us/dotnet/visual-basic/language-reference/data-types/data-type-summary) describes the various fully supported data types.

Visual Basic type	Common language runtime type structure	Nominal storage allocation	Value range
Boolean	Boolean	Depends on implementing platform	`True` or `False`
Byte	Byte	1 byte	0 through 255 (unsigned)
Char (single character)	Char	2 bytes	0 through 65535 (unsigned)
Date	DateTime	8 bytes	0:00:00 (midnight) on January 1, 0001 through 11:59:59 PM on December 31, 9999
Decimal	Decimal	16 bytes	0 through +/- 79,228,162,514,264,337,593,543,950,335 (+/- 7.9...E+28) ꞌ with no decimal point; 0 through +/- 7.9228162514264337593543950335 with 28 places to the right of the decimal; smallest nonzero number is +/- 0.0000000000000000000000000001 (+/-1E-28) ꞌ
Double (double-	Double	8 bytes	-1.79769313486231570E+308 through -4.94065645841246544E-324 ꞌ for negative values;

Visual Basic type	Common language runtime type structure	Nominal storage allocation	Value range
precision floating-point)			4.94065645841246544E-324 through 1.79769313486231570E+308 ˙ for positive values
Integer	Int32	4 bytes	-2,147,483,648 through 2,147,483,647 (signed)
Long (long integer)	Int64	8 bytes	-9,223,372,036,854,775,808 through 9,223,372,036,854,775,807 (9.2...E+18 ˙) (signed)
Object	Object (class)	4 bytes on 32-bit platform 8 bytes on 64-bit platform	Any type can be stored in a variable of type `Object`
SByte	SByte	1 byte	-128 through 127 (signed)
Short (short integer)	Int16	2 bytes	-32,768 through 32,767 (signed)
Single (single-precision floating-	Single	4 bytes	-3.4028235E+38 through -1.401298E-45 ˙ for negative values; 1.401298E-45 through 3.4028235E+38 ˙ for

Visual Basic type	Common language runtime type structure	Nominal storage allocation	Value range
point)			positive values
String (variable-length)	String (class)	Depends on implementing platform	0 to approximately 2 billion Unicode characters
UInteger	UInt32	4 bytes	0 through 4,294,967,295 (unsigned)
ULong	UInt64	8 bytes	0 through 18,446,744,073,709,551,615 (1.8...E+19) (unsigned)
User-Defined (structure)	(inherits from ValueType)	Depends on implementing platform	Each member of the structure has a range determined by its data type and independent of the ranges of the other members
UShort	UInt16	2 bytes	0 through 65,535 (unsigned)

Installing Visual Studio at home

The Community edition of Visual Studio is a free download and install so if you have a Windows 10 computer at home you can install it for your own use. This is valuable if you want to try some additional things, experiment with your code outside of school. Or continue learning after your course is over.

1. Go to https://www.visualstudio.com/vs/community/
2. Download VS Community 2017
3. Select Keep for the warning that pops up
4. Run the exe file that downloads
5. Click Continue to accept the license terms
   It is always wise to read through license terms for software you install. It may be boring but you need to know what you are agreeing to.
6. Here are the Workloads that I install for the course:

   You can add more if they look interesting but they well take up more room on disk and make the installation take longer.
7. Installation will take a while! Make sure your computer is plugged in and won't go into sleep mode.

Index

Arrays, 38
    declaring, 38
    initialize, 38
    Length property, 39
    Methods, 39
    Properties, 39
ASCII, 13
assignment operator, 14
Boolean, 11, 12, 13, 23, 24, 27, 28, 29, 56
Boolean expressions, 23
case sensitive., 11
Classes
    Definition, 47
Close, 36
Collisions, 55
Constructors, 48
control value, 39
counter variable, 28
Creating Event Handlers, 53, 63
design window, 5, 9, 52
Dialog Box
    Return value, 33
    SaveFileDialog, 34
DialogResult, 33
Double, 8, 11, 12, 16, 26, 32, 59
ElseIf, 25
Event handler, 8
event handlers, 46, 47
exponentiation, 10
file
    Checking for more data, 35
    Close, 35
    Reading, 34
files, 32
    Reading, 34
Files
    Flush, 36
    StreamWriter, 35
    Writing, 35
floating point numbers, 12
Flush, 36
Fort property, 7
helper methods, 49
IDE, 4, 11
index values, 38
IndexOf
    String, 19
infinite loop, 29

instantiation, 47
integer, 12, 14, 52
Length property, 39
loops
   essential components, 27, 28
Mathematical Operators, 10
Menu object, 58
methods
   Helper, 49
name property, 7
object
   Definition, 47
Object
   Creation. *See* instantiation
Objects
   Declaring, 50
Open File Dialog, 56
OpenFileDialog, 33, 34
parameters, 18, 19, 21, 23, 41, 43, 47
parse, 22
Peek, 35
Properties
   Of Objects, 49
Random, 11, 12, 13, 14
Random numbers, 13
Read, 34
ReadLine, 34
Rectangle, 55, 56
SaveFileDialog, 34
scope of variables, 66
sequential files, 32
ShowDialog
   OpenFileDialog, 33
Split method, 20
StreamReader, 34
StreamWriter, 35
   Write, 36
   WriteLine, 36
string
   Formatting, 21
String
   Converting to number, 22
   IndexOf, 19
   Length, 18
   Parse, 22
   Split, 20
   Split Method, 20
   Substring, 18

   ToLower, 19
   ToUpper, 19
   TryParse, 23
Strings, 12, 13, 17
text property, 7, 17, 61
timer, 52
toolbox, 5
ToString, 17, 20, 21, 22
TryParse, 23
Unicode, 13
Val function, 17, 26, 32
Variable, 10, 11
WriteLine, 36

www.ingramcontent.com/pod-product-compliance
Lightning Source LLC
Chambersburg PA
CBHW060204060326
40690CB00018B/4246